Hold That Joan

THE LIFE, LAUGHS AND FILMS OF JOAN DAVIS

BY BEN OHMART

Ben Ohmart

HOLD THAT JOAN: THE LIFE, LAUGHS AND FILMS OF JOAN DAVIS
© 2007 Ben Ohmart

PUBLISHED IN THE USA BY:

BearManor Media
PO Box 71426
Albany, GA 31708
www.BearManorMedia.com

LIBRARY OF CONGRESS CATALOGING-IN-PUBLICATION DATA:

Ohmart, Ben.
 Hold that Joan : the life, laughs and films of Joan Davis / by Ben Ohmart.
     p. cm.
 Includes index.
 ISBN-13: 978-1-59393-046-2
 1. Davis, Joan, 1912-1961. 2. Actors--United States--Biography. I. Title.

PN2287.D3216O46 2007
792.02'8092--dc22
 [B]
                                        2006030438
Printed in the United States.

Design and Layout by Valerie Thompson.

Table of Contents

For Ron Wright

and

Charles Stumpf

Without you, my friends, there would be no book

Introduction

Unless time travel becomes a fact of life, a *complete* book on Joan Davis can never be. The fire that once destroyed part of Joan's home, and another that tragically took the lives of her remaining family, also unfortunately claimed the treasures of full knowledge. A lifetime of scrapbooks, rare, irreplaceable family photos, information & heirlooms from the Davis family legacy—all gone too quickly, too horribly. That's why critics may scoff at the final chapter—that it is too abrupt, the soup too thin, but I suffered from the same nutritionally skimpy malady that plagued my Walter Tetley book. Lots of information on his and Joan's early life, but very little when the spotlights began to dim. What you read here is as close as I could get to the truth without firsthand knowledge.

Joan with an early family album.

Therefore, when reading this treatise, it may also feel as if the opening chapter has gone missing. However, after researching for a while, I came to the conclusion that giving this project more time would be like waiting for a bus on a desert island. Of course if significant information comes along because of this book (it happened after I wrote the Paul Frees biography, so it's possible), I'm certainly game to update the work appropriately. This book is mainly based upon the wealth of magazine articles on Joan throughout the years (some notoriously fabricated, the creative dreams from teams of press reporters seeking a sensationalist angle) and other sources, and while you should take some of it with a grain of salt, I did not salt the soup too much, don't worry.

I did uncover two main witnesses—daughter Beverly's first husband, Lee Bamber, and penultimate husband, Alan Grossman, who shed a very alternative light onto what is otherwise a respectful, impartially positive biography. While there may be bias in these interviews and though true JD fans may cringe and question the several insights they offer here, for the sake of completeness and objective reporting, I felt it only right to include the little first-hand material that was available. However, when taken alongside the comments of Jim Backus in his autobiography, a very different concept of Joan Davis begins to emerge.

Regardless of the true Joan Davis, I am a fan first and foremost. To me, she was funnier than Lucy, one of the greatest comediennes filmdom has ever captured, and could wring a solid yuk out of just a slippery floor or a man-hungry line. She was *brilliant*. And far too often underused in her films. And could upstage anyone, *anyone*, if she put her squeaky-voiced mind to it. But she never tried to upstage during her years as a supporting player at 20th Century-Fox. Her only ambition was comic perfection.

In the only other lengthy treatise written on this great pratfalling talent, James Robert Parish wrote in **The Slapstick Queens** that "Joan Davis was one of the few comediennes of all time to have appealed both to the intellectuals and the masses." Jimmy Fidler of the **San Francisco Chronicle** once wrote, "In-a-word description of Joan Davis' acting: Super-facial." She played for laughs, and she mugged to milk them harder. She never aimed to be a star or actress of "heavy drama." She was beautiful, but not glamorous, lanky, but balanced. Thank God she remained Joan Davis . . .

As the dedication clearly indicates, there would be no book without the relentless help of the premiere Joan Davis collector in the world, Ron Wright. He let me rifle through his deep and jaw-dropping JD files and pictures, letting me borrow whatever took my fancy. Though distance was a problem, I ultimately purloined a ton of material for this book, much of which I doubt I could've duplicated even three years later with dedicated research. You saved me—and the readers—a good five years, Ron, and I will be eternally grateful for your generosity.

A sincere, special thanks also goes out to the man who made my connection with Ron possible—a true collector, gentleman, and *sincere* lover of old films and the great character people of the 20th century. Charles Stumpf has helped me more with books, contacts, information and just plain support than any other person, and his dedication to the field of old movies have always been an inspiration to me. Thanks, Charles.

And to Lee Bamber, Beverly's ex-husband and one of the very few first-hand witnesses I could locate. You shed invaluable light on the Davis/Wills household and were very generous with your time and stories. It makes me wonder what kind of book this would have been—good or bad, juicy or damaging—if Bev, Si or just one of the main characters of Joan's life had been around to interview.

And a special thanks to Laura Wagner, without whose consistent help, photos, tireless energy and brilliance I would be simply a blind and wandering man.

There are lots of others to thank: for invaluable help with *I Married Joan* specifics, The Classic TV Archive (http://www.geocities.com/TelevisionCity/Stage/2950/), run by Des Martin, with contributions by Jim Brent, Tom Alger, Wayne Miller, John King and Revel Partington; Hayden Jameson (for important research on Joan's high school years); G.D. Hamann, for your impressive collection of books of Los Angeles newspaper film reviews; Dee DeTevis for generously sharing her *I Married Joan* shows with me (and other fans); Sandy Singer; Martin Grams, Jr., for an unending stream of radio assistance; William Bast; and Alan Grossman, for coming forward at the last minute and making this book richer because of it.

And thank you, Mayu, for always being there, supportive and loving to the last.

BEN OHMART
MARCH 2006

Chapter 1
Little Jo

Not too much is known about Joan's ethnic origins or parents. Her father, LeRoy Davis, was a train dispatcher for Northern Pacific, who married Nina Davis at the turn of the 20th century.

Joan and her father in 1948.

Madonna Josephine Davis, soon called just "Jo," was born on June 29, 1912 in St. Paul, Minnesota. Her grandfather played the bass fiddle in a small orchestra, and that seemed to be the extent of the theatrical bug biting the family tree.

Living across the street from a school, pre-kindergarten Joan would watch the kids try out the horizontal bars and athletic equipment, and she would often toddle over to emulate the fun. When she fell and a passerby would laugh, it only inspired her to fall more often. Inducing the kids to laughter encouraged Joan to try harder pieces of business. Even early on, she liked the sound of guffaws.

She told *Woman's Home Companion* years later, "Some girls are born with a face like a doll's and fall right into show business off a drugstore stool. Not me. The only falling I did was off the railing of the school—when I was mugging my three-year-old best to attract an audience. Kindergarten looked like the big time then and I was still too young to make it. I was crazy for an audience. I was crazy."

At the bruised and tender age of three, Jo was already singing, dancing and reciting at various local gatherings. Just a few years later, at one of these recitations, her life and career was changed forever when she collected her first, unintentional, laugh from a seated audience. According to other reports, she narrowly missed a bushel's worth of rotten vegetables, so generously thrown by booing fans. It may have been the origin of her gawky, swinging legs when her father advised, "Joan, you lay beautiful eggs. Better be funny, not serious, keep moving. It spoils their aim!"

Switching her presentation to a comedy act a week later at that same theater earned her hoots and excited applause. Already cultivating the image of a skinny, maladroit girl, one of her most successful routines had Jo flying around as Cupid with a painted, gilded coat hanger for a bow. Her stage persona was already on the make for a man . . .

Another version of comical Joan's origin had little six-year-old Josephine singing, with plenty of elaborate, ill-timed facial expressions:

I AIN'T NOBODY'S DARLING, I'M JUST
AS BLUE AS CAN BE,
BECAUSE I AIN'T GOT NOBODY TO MAKE
A FUSS OVER ME.
IF I DON'T GET SOMEBODY, I'LL GO
BACK TO THE FARM
AND MILK THE COWS AND CHICKENS,
BECAUSE THEY DON'T GIVE A DARN.

After her parents instantly learned that the audience wasn't laughing with but *at* their daughter, they dressed her in a short blue dress, green bloomers that fell to her ankles, and a straw hat. It was the same principle stand-up comics use even today: give them a *reason* to laugh at you, then it's okay when they do.

"I first knew this show-business life was strictly for me when I was six and faced that first audience," said Joan. "I remember the feel of them, the people out there, waiting for me. I sang a straight song and danced a straight dance with high kicks. Nothing. I laid an egg big enough to hurt my feelings for a long time.

Dad's feelings were hurt too. That was my first and last straight act. 'Okay, honey,' Dad said, 'do it your way. Be funny.' I wore an apron, a pair of Grandpa's gaiters, sang 'I Ain't Nobody's Darling' and 'Sweet Hortense.' No more eggs. In fact, I began to earn money, $4 for each first place in amateur-night contests."

By the time she was eight, she had won 27 first-place contests in Seattle, including a Washington State championship.

A very young Joan Davis.

Joan herself later gave yet another version to the 20th Century-Fox publicity department: "I guess my first appearance as an actress was at the age of three when Mom encouraged me to sing in church. And by the time I was seven, I was sure and Pop was willing to be convinced that I was ready for my debut. It was at an amateur night performance at a movie—and I'll never forget it. What I sang there was something to the effect that 'like sunbeams need the sunshine, like roses need the dew, like a baby needs its mother, that's how I need you.' Because nobody stopped me in the middle of the song, I figured the prize was already in the bag for baby Joan. But when the manager held his hand over my head, asking the audience's opinion of my little labor of love, the only applause I received was from the one who is still my staunchest fan—my dad! Mom had remained at home—she had stage fright, or maybe she anticipated what would happen.

"On the way home Dad put his arm around me, and said consolingly, 'Joan, I guess you're just not cut out for the stage.' And although I sobbed in reply that I was inclined to agree with his notion of my failure as an actress, when I got to thinking the matter over, I decided that my failure lay not in myself as a potential stage success, but in my choice of a role. There and then I decided that if I couldn't roll them into the aisles—which is just an expression, for I never saw it happen—as a straight actress or songbird, maybe I could make people laugh. So a few nights later when there was another amateur show at a picture-house, I tried a comedy song. It won me the first prize, and from then on I did pretty well at amateur nights, by kidding myself and the world with me."

Soon she impressed vaudeville scouts in the audience, who urged the child's parents to let Jo tour on their Pantages Theater Circuit, signed up by Alexander Pantages himself. One 1937 report from Hollywood claimed that Joan's parents passed up an opportunity from Sid Grauman for her to join the Our Gang (Little Rascals) team, while in a 1954 interview, Joan herself stated, "We decided to try

Los Angeles where Pantages and Grauman were sponsoring tryouts. Pantages signed me for his vaudeville circuit—and the next day—too late—Sid Grauman called, wanting me for *Our Gang* movies. That was life's darkest moment. Dad and Mother were heartbroken right along with me, there in our little rooming-house room. We didn't know that this was a lucky break; as a child movie actress, I'd probably have had only a brief career, while vaudeville gave me long hard years of training."

She developed her fourteen-minute act as "The Toy Comedienne" and sometimes the "Cyclonic Josephine Davis." Accompanied by her mother and a tutor on the road, whenever possible Mom made sure she was taken back to St. Paul for a few months' schooling. She did an "underdressed act," but "I was no striptease artiste. Underdressed meant that I wore seven changes of costume all at once, hurried into the wings after each song or recitation, peeled off one and exposed another until I didn't look quite so overstuffed." She recited and sang songs like "I'm Silly Milly," "I Ain't Nobody's Darling" and "You Tell 'Em, I Stutter." When playing a New York theater, her parents called her a midget, to avoid child labor laws. Only when the manager spotted her wearing a child's Munsing underwear was she thrown out.

"At the ripe old age of eight," Joan later joked, "came my first thought of retiring. My parents and I were walking my toy Boston terrier Jaydee after the late show one evening and dropped in at an all-night delicatessen. Jaydee took one delicious whiff, showed her teeth and distinctly said, 'Mama. Mama.' A talking dog! I could retire and make a fortune! I dangled every tantalizing possibility under that dog's nose every day of her life but she never spoke again. I had to keep on working."

She was learning a great deal about pleasing audiences and already assembling an impressive joke catalog. But after a few years of touring, the Davises knew that the road was no place to learn everything, and the uncertainty of an actor's life really required something to fall back on. She was also outgrowing her original act, and as a seasoned sixteen-year-old, retired the act to further her education.

Where she finished her elementary education is uncertain, but in June of 1927 Josephine Davis was listed as a Freshman in her G.W. (George Weitbrecht) Mechanic Arts High School yearbook (known as "The M"). As of January of that year she was already on the Student Council and part of the newly-formed Debating Club. She was placed on the first team with three other girls, and became one of its stars. Naturally. She once held the affirmative position on "We Should Abolish Capital Punishment" and won the judges' vote. She was also involved in sports: on the track team, she was labeled "the human deer."

Of course, she was also involved in school theatre productions. She was one of the Three Little Maids in *The Mikado*, and played an old washerwoman in another show, keeping the girls entertained with specialty numbers during intermission. Though she never took a dancing lesson in her life, she also taught the kids dance numbers for some of the musical shows.

Debating Club. Joan is 3rd from right, front row.

At some point around this time Joan was in the Girl Reserves, which had its membership party at the YWCA, and taught "politeness and poise, education and efficiency, resourcefulness and reliability, service and sacrifice, and optimism and objectivity." For one special assembly the Girl Reserves joined with the Girls' Cogwheel Club for a Washington's Birthday celebration on February 21, 1927, in which "Josephine Davis danced the minuet in costume."

The Girls' Cogwheel Club. Joan is 3rd from right, front row.

As a member of the Student Council, she was once honored with a school assembly for having straight A's, even though she was working nearly every night in various stage entertainments.

Josephine Davis, far left of front row, in the Student Council.

She was not listed at all in the 1930 yearbook, the year she would have graduated, which makes one wonder if she completed high school. After all, this was the year she began making headway on the stage. One source states that she graduated as valedictorian of her class. Years later, Joan said, "I kept on going to school a season, then working [acting] a season. I was crazy about school and had a solid A report card all through Mechanical Arts High School. At least I thought it was a solid A until my daughter Beverly went to St. Paul two years ago [1952] to visit Dad. She looked up the records and found I'd had one B. She's never let me forget it."

Joan decided to try the real world for a change and earned a whopping $8 a week at the local Five-and-Dime, where she sold goldfish. She would frequently ask buyers, "Would you like this wrapped as a gift?" and keep in step with an impromptu rubbery leg routine, sliding around the floor. It was no use. Even a transfusion would not remove show business.

But as Joan said in a 1954 interview, "I was still in high school when next I decided to retire. I was touring with an act called 'School Days' but my heart was back home in St. Paul with my first beau, Jim. I wrote to him every night and yearned to get back to him. One day, at the Palace Theatre in Chicago, I was going to my desk on stage when I was handed a letter. It was from Jim and I couldn't wait, I opened it behind a book right there on stage. 'Dear Joan,' Jim wrote, 'I've found another girl. You're never home and . . .'

"Then and there I hated show business. I'd give it up forever the minute the season was over. I did too. I decided on a business career and started at the bottom, the dime store in St. Paul. I was put behind the goldfish counter. Ever try catching a goldfish?"

While working at Kress' dime store on 7th Street in Minneapolis, "I got $12 a week for peddling goldfish. But at the end of two weeks, I felt I couldn't stand the work any longer. One morning as I was walking down to the basement, I saw a mop standing in a pail, beside a soapy place on the floor. In fact, I was so busy watching that bucket and thinking that a scrubwoman couldn't work half as hard as I, that I slipped on the soapy floor. I did a skid on one of my French heels and landed kerplunk on the back part of my stomach, where it hurts the worst. I felt pretty sore when I got up, and I didn't make any bones about complaining to the management. They sent me to the hospital and I stayed there two weeks—on salary and with all expenses paid. It was the first real rest I'd had in years, and that accident taught me the fall-gag which for the past few years has been my bread, butter and beans."

No sooner was she released from school—and goldfish— that she decided to extend her *real* education immediately and took to the vaudeville stage once again, moonlighting between an old act while spending her off-hours learning new routines and developing her timing and skills by watching the other acts in the house. She also enjoyed studying Charlie Chaplin films, particularly his quirky, sometimes stiffly lanky nature and naturalness at taking a pratfall. She learned a good lesson in mugging from the master silent clown, incorporating the best of slapstick with her squeaky, almost deadpan monotones of patter. One such physical part of her act included a gravity-defying juggling bit in which a huge stack of dishes never quite seemed to topple.

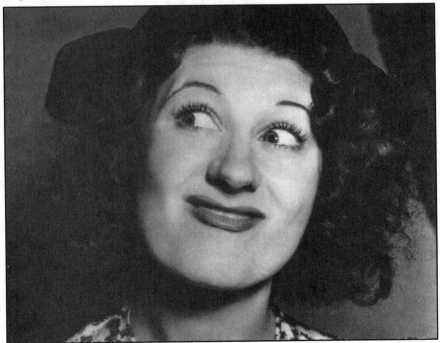

No beer has a better mug.

"I studied the technique of every stage and screen comedian," Joan told reporters later, "analyzing the slightest differences. I prefer the sympathetic type of comedy that carries the elements of surprise. I make my comedy seem accidental and I like to have my audiences think 'poor girl, she tries so hard and everything goes wrong.'"

While still a teenager Joan played nearly every vaudeville circuit in the United States, as well as amusement parks, summer camps, Elks lodges, any festivity that paid for a laugh. Never one to keep rehashing the same material indefinitely (even if it worked every time), Joan and her manager had considered adding a straight man to the act to unchain the comic possibilities. A young actor by the name of Serenus "Si" Wills was also seeking a partner.

Meeting on St. Patrick's Day, 1931 (some reports state it was March 17), the two were an obvious comedic match. Si was a veteran of the vaudeville stage, typical of the hoke comic of the day: putty nose, ill-fitting trousers. When he first met his would-be partner, "I almost died when she showed up. In her act she wore green ruffled drawers down to her ankles and a hat even a queen wouldn't be seen in."

In an article ("I Married a Straight Woman") by Si around 1957, he stated, "It all began around 1930. I was in vaudeville at the time. I was looking for a straight man at the time and Joan was looking for a partner. It was inevitable we should meet. After three weeks of teaming together, I played straight man and Joan took over the gags. She was a natural comic."

A March 1, 1966 letter from Si to comedy writer Billy Glason further paints his god-like view of the relationship: "Good old vaudeville—those were the carefree days. I love to

Si Wills

reminisce about it. On my first trip to California I fell in love with it, and vowed that someday, I would live there permanently. In New York, I was signed to write and star in some two-reel comedies. Then when I finished the series there, the company sent me to Calif. to make another series. When I finished that series, I went back into vaudeville and put Joan in my act. After a year we got married. Then we were going to have a baby, so I decided that she should have the baby in Calif., and I would work in pictures. After working in pictures for four years

I got Joan a job in pictures, and got her a seven-year contract. I did all the comedy writing for her. Then I got her a radio program and supervised the writing for that show. Joan got too big and we decided to get a divorce (1948) but we remained very close friends. I continued to write for her. My last writing efforts were all the story lines for two years, for the *I Married Joan* television show series."

In a later interview, Joan told of how "I started working with Si Wills, a comedian. Our opening night in Rutherford, New Jersey, was one for the books. I had told Si that I had a beautiful wardrobe. What I had were old broken-down comedy clothes—big shoes, funny hat, umbrella and the checked gingham dress I'd worn for years. I came out shyly, wondering how he'd take it. Then out came Si, just as funny-looking as I! We looked at each other and howled, the audience howled too. We were in.

"Of course we fell in love almost right away. We talked it over, agreed that love would spoil our act, we'd be sensible, we'd be friends and partners . . . In five months, we were married."

Actually, it was a whirlwind courtship. According to one article, Si fell in love first, but had to contend with Joan's career; he won her by slipping a diamond ring on her finger and giving her a cactus plant to take care of. The couple had only known each other five months, performing as "Wills and Davis," when they got married in Chicago on August 13 or 31, 1931. Like true troupers, they honeymooned on the road, while performing in Cedar Point, Ohio. For booking and billing reasons, Joan kept her maiden name. For the next few years they toured and barnstormed their way up to the pinnacle of many a vaudeville team's dream: the Palace Theatre in New York City. Occasionally Joan would fill up her odd time on the road with some compulsive poker playing with other acts and stage hands, usually ending up as the loser of the night and putting the Wills family in a hard luck position.

On October 19, 1931, they performed on the same bill with singer/dancer James Barton. *The New York Times* called them a "highly promising team." In the week of September 29, 1933 Joan, Si and others "assisted" Ed Lowry and his band on stage to support the Will Rogers film *Dr. Bull* at Loew's State Theater. *The Los Angeles Illustrated News* proclaimed that the duo "convulsed the audience with their comedy antics." They were making $1500 a week as headliners around this point, great money then *and* now.

Though other reviews of their act were dated 1932, constant mention to Joan's film work suggests that they were still performing together onstage after 1935. One Philadelphia newspaper stated they are "hardly a new act, having been known in vaude a good many years ago as Davis and Wills. Formerly the act was Wills'; now Miss Davis is the sparkling one. It's a socko turn, one of the most entertaining seen in months from a film name. In this case, it's not merely a matter of 'I'm from Hollywood. Look at me in the flesh.' Reminiscent of the halcyon vaude days, the act is packed with material, is funny on its own, and nicely timed and routined.

"Wills comes on first, after a build-up as a local boy, which in this case happens to be true. He brings Miss Davis on and they go through some Dumb Dora patter. She then sings tunes from her pix. With her exit Wills goes into a straight gag routine, using a balloon as a crystal ball. Some of his stuff is pretty blue, though not offensive, and of varying degrees of value. Miss Davis comes back to do a stint of her nutty terping, slides and falls. After numerous encores she intros Wills as her husband in a nice speech, gets in a couple more gags and is off for a neat finale."

An early photo of Si and Joan in Hollywood, before she became a blonde.

When sharing the bill with Dolores Del Rio's picture, *Girl of the Rio*, at the RKO Orpheum Theater in the middle of January 1932, the Wills/Davis combo was reported to be "A Youthful Fit of Wit. First, last and always they are for fun, and whether singing, dancing, talking or engaging in some bit of hokum business, comedy is their sole purpose."

"For the third time," said Joan later, "I decided to retire. I was married now—I'd retire, start keeping house, have kids. The team of Wills and Davis, however, needed a quick few thousand for furniture, so we knocked off one quick booking.

"About this time, Arthur Willis of RKO spotted us for the Palace—the big time then for all vaudeville performers. He said, 'You're a funny act but—you'll have to clean up the girl.' I was crushed. I didn't know what he meant. He meant that the comedy clothes and well-fed look must go. Davis must wear evening clothes and be glamorous.

"I fought it tooth and nail. I was used to getting laughs by catching my hat as it fell, by holding my umbrella straight in the air. How could I be funny without props? But the Palace was waiting for us, the big time, the two-a-day. Mecca. They broke me in gradually on the circuit. One night when I started to dress, my long green drawers were gone. The next night my checkered dress was gone. In its place was a lovely evening gown. I wore it but I clung to my big shoes, my hat and my umbrella. Then the shoes were gone. I had to wear high heels and I fell all over. Then the hat disappeared. I clutched my umbrella as long as I could. Then it was gone too.

"Now it was Si's turn. He almost flipped when they told him to dress straight. Once or twice, casing an audience, seeing how tough they were, we'd sneak back into our old clothes. But we got the word fast: no more old clothes or we'd be fired from the RKO circuit.

"However, except for our clothes, our act was unchanged. We had a fast cornball routine with jokes delivered at machine-gun speed. Finally, we reached the Palace. I wore a light blue gown with mink sleeves and collar, very expensive, probably $75 or $100. I dressed and sauntered out into the wings. Then suddenly, waiting for our music, fear hit me for the first time in my life. I could see the dark sea of waiting people. *This* was the Palace, this could make or break you, this was important! I was almost paralyzed I was so scared, even through the applause, even though we were a hit. Stage fright and stage-struck, I guess, go together.

"Si and I toured all over during the next years. Every once in a while I thought of retiring. Once when we were on tour down south, I did quit. I was tired and tired of show business. But Si got so many laughs alone, it killed me and I went back to work the next day. I was hooked for good, although I still hadn't given up the hope of quitting. I didn't know then that the only other time I'd take time off would be when Beverly was born. Out of a marriage like Si's and mine, Beverly was a natural. Ever since she could walk or talk, she was stage-struck, too."

Beverly Wills was born on June 7, 1934 (some references state August 5, 1933). Si explained, "We went on touring vaudeville and were set to go abroad when we discovered our baby was on the way. That decided our moving to California where I had some work for Mack Sennett and others.

"Following Beverly's birth Joan and I decided it was time we settled down, and so our traveling was somewhat curtailed. We still made theatrical appearances across the country."

The Wills family, posed at home.

Joan: "Beverly made her stage debut at the age of ten weeks. We were touring then, and one of the acts featured Barbara Stanwyck [in Boston]. One night during a curtain call, she carried Bev onto the stage. Bev took to it and has been acting ever since. By the time she was three, for the last couple years she worked as a sort of tag to our act, imitating me. She had started copying my routines from the time she could walk, just by watching. Our traveling gear always included a case of condensed milk. I used to throw disposable diapers out of train windows, heat Bev's bottle on a portable stove and squeeze orange juice as the train rocked.

"Bev made her *real* debut at three. We were breaking in an act at Long Beach. Si and I had taken our bows and were headed for the basement dressing rooms when we heard the band break into a tune we used, 'Alexander's Ragtime Band.' We scrambled back upstairs and there in the center of the stage was Beverly. She'd scooted out and introduced herself.

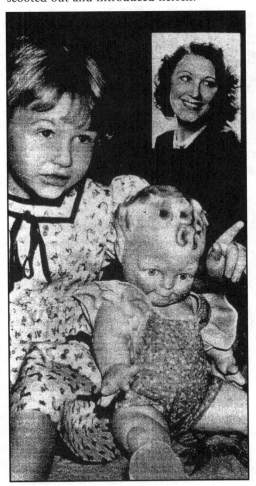

Beverly Wills

"'What do you want, dear?' the unsuspecting emcee had asked.

"'I want to sing Alexander's Ragtime Band.'

"And she sang. And the house came down. From then on we couldn't trust her in the wings without shackles. We gave her a bit with us to keep her from total frustration.

"Also, we used to have to watch her or she'd walk into someone else's act. One night she went out on the stage and messed up the magician's act—got into a cage and let the pigeons and rabbits loose. The audience went wild, but it was pretty tough on the magician."

Beverly later recalled, "When I was five years old we did one of those routines that went something like this: 'What's your name, little girl?'—'Beverly.'—'How old are you?'—'Five.'—'Who is your mother?'—'My mother is the funniest, the most wonderful actress in the world—isn't that what you told me to say, Mommy?' And then I got pulled off the stage by my ear."

When the time came for Beverly to start school, the team of Davis & Wills quit the road. With the vaudeville stage shakily on the wane due to the increased competition of films and radio on the public's attention, Joan and Si took the view of "if you can't beat them, join them." The family headed out West and bought a house in Beverly Hills (which they lived in for years), which they christened "The House of All Nations," because of its Moorish architecture and each room flaunting the style of a different country, many of which the young couple hoped to visit someday. There was a Turkish dining room, a Spanish living room, a South Seas playroom, a Hawaiian bar, a French bedroom, a Swedish bedroom, but only Joan's own bedroom was, as she called it, a "Hollywood-American-glamour-gal bedroom." Upstairs were separate bedrooms for Si, Joan and Beverly, and a guestroom. A "playhouse" was soon built for Bev: a miniature version of a real house, with a small picket fence in front.

A young Beverly.

Now that she was looking to conquer the coast, Joan liked seeing herself in tailored suits—blue was her best color. She was the opposite of her screen persona when the cameras were off; she had an elegance and controlled class that were nearer her true nature than simply a class clown. Joan made the rounds of producers, playing, with Si, all the nightclubs they could find to drum up interest in this new town. She was told that she should initially offer a free bit in a picture, just to have a routine on film, but even that took some doing with cold auditions.

After getting no further than the reception desk at Education Films (known for its popular one- and two-reelers that supported feature films), Joan decided to get ahead the true Hollywood way. She threw a party. She stocked her audience with old vaudeville friends who knew just where to laugh and holler and applaud while she did her after-dinner schtick. Joan knew that slapstick king Mack Sennett was directing a production for Educational (and it would be his last for that studio), and so devised an entire night of Joan Davis showcasing, expending literally her entire repertoire to impress the legendary director. It worked. Even though the next day Sennett's secretary stopped her cold with the words that she was too old for the role they were thinking of, Joan promptly returned the next morning in bow, short skirt, curled hair and starched blouse—everything but a yo-yo. She was in.

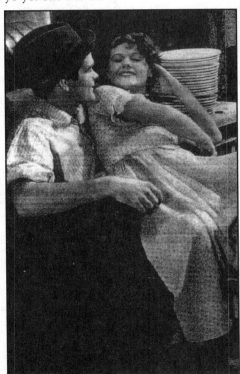

Way Up Thar.

The 20-minute short was *Way Up Thar*, based on a story by Olive Hatch, in which Joan plays Jenny Kirk, part of a family of Ozark bumpkins who hanker to be radio singers. If ever there was a commercial for the Joan Davis style, this was it. She was blessed with enough time to repeat her famous balancing dishes routine, and sang "Comin' Round the Mountain," "I'm Gonna Get Married" and "That's Why I Stutter." She could not have asked for a better introduction to film audiences. Especially since she shared the screen with the popular Western song group, The Sons of the Pioneers (with Roy Rogers). The short was produced and directed by Sennett and was released on November 8, 1935. It was later included in the compilation films *Birth of a Star* (1945) and *The Sound of Laughter* (1963).

In an interview, Joan stated, "It ran for a day and a half, including all night. Buster Keaton's mother played my mother in it. I was so worn out before I was through. I told Si, 'If this is the movies, get me out of them, I've aged so since yesterday I won't match in the rushes.'"

Si and Joan were still a team, at least professionally, in the late 1930s after Joan had her film contract. Si recalled, "She used to bring her scripts home to me. Together we'd work out routines. I became her writer, and today, along with two others, I'm working on CBS' *Joannie's Tea Room*."

RKO was very interested in her, and offered her a contract that did nothing for her career. Eyeing her for a collection of shorts—since she obviously excelled at short-spurt comedy—they kept her as a contract player for four months, only using her once.

Bunker Bean, which opened in New York on June 26, 1936, was the third screen version of Harry Leon Wilson's novel about a timid stenographer who is convinced he's the reincarnation of someone powerful (Napoleon or Egyptian pharaoh Ram Tah, perhaps). The film starred Owen Davis, Jr., as the lead character, and had a young Lucille Ball in a small part, while Joan was apparently cast as the telephone operator, though she doesn't appear on screen.

About all Joan did at RKO was pose for pictures.

Failing to find a proper vehicle for her, RKO did not fight Joan's wanting out of her contract, which ended in the latter part of 1935.

To fill in a little time, she did a favor for Si's close friend, director Ray McCarey, (and herself) by singing "You Tell Her Because I Stutter" in Paramount Pictures' *Millions in the Air*, a musical based on the very popular Major Bowes radio amateur hour. The 1935 film starred John Howard, Wendy Barrie and Robert Cummings. As with many films trying to replicate the success of radio, it didn't quite work, but, like a good vaudeville movie, allowed ample room for comedy, singing and (not too smart for radio) dancing.

Failing to conquer Hollywood, Joan and family moved back east, securing a place on the stage of the illustrious Palace Theater on Broadway. Unfortunately, it seemed luck had forsaken Joan in this pivotal part of her life. The Wills/Davis team bombed. Even with the negative publicity, however, they managed to land enough theaters for a continued tour of vaudeville for the next six months. Joan was keeping up with her Hollywood friends on her off-hours, though.

20th Century-Fox, always on the lookout for new talent, was wanting to expand their comedy and musical offerings, and inveigled Joan with a long-term contract by long distance. Back to California . . .

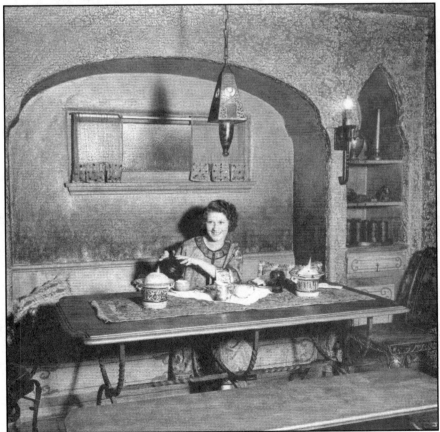

At home in the early 1930s.

Chapter 2

A Cameo Career

*T*he *Holy Terror* (1937), no relation to Fox's previous *A Holy Terror* (1931),
was based on a Fox-owned Winchell Smith/George Abbott play. It was an
amusing, though completely mistitled 67-minute musical, starring Jane Withers,
Tony Martin and Leah Ray, filmed between late October and late November
1936, and generally devoid of Davis, save for one capricious song near the end.

Corky Wallace (Jane Withers), daughter of Lt. Commandar Wallace (John
Elredge), always seems to find herself annoying U.S. Navy Commander, Capt.
J.J. Otis (Andrew Tombes), but has befriended seaman Danny Walker (Tony
Martin), who is in love with the owner of the Golden Anchor café, Marjorie
Dean (Leah Ray). Lil (Joan Davis) is the café's cook and dish washer with a stutter
that can only be cured with a good sock in the jaw. When spies find out about
the Navy's new planes (photos of which would interest other countries), they
make a plan to close the café, which is in a perfect location from which to spy.
They begin a riot during a show there, forcing the Navy to close the Golden
Anchor and arrest the men involved. Only through the devious cuteness of Corky
are the men released just in time to foil the spy plot and rescue the kidnapped
Margorie and Lil, who, during the final fight between sailors and spies, conks
everyone on the head she can with a frying pan.

The New York Times wrote that Joan is a "strange female curtain-climber, with
a trick of punching herself in the jaw and a curious resemblance to Olive Oyl in
the cartoons."

On the Avenue (1937) was chock-full of Irving Berlin songs (notably "I've Got
My Love to Keep Me Warm") and just about all of the best talent on the Fox lot.
Under the working title of *Out Front*, Berlin was paid an astonishing $75,000
plus 10% of the gross proceeds to write songs for this film. There wasn't much
plot to the 90-minute revue. So? With Alice Faye and Dick Powell on hand for
singing and the Ritz Brothers on foot for loads of extreme absurdity, a slight love
plot between Powell and Madeleine Carroll and plenty of production numbers
were all that were needed. Again, not much Joan in this one—she played a
secretary—but it was a start.

The Hollywood publicity machine began to run for Joan Davis, press releases
beginning to crank out like confetti. According to studio publicity at the time,

A rare wardrobe test for *The Holy Terror*, 1937.

Joan's hobbies included riding three times a week, bowling, tennis, swimming and playing golf. Her favorite scent was Tou Jours Moi; her customary superstition, knocking on wood; her favorite flower, the peony; favorite color, cerise; favorite writer, Gene Fowler; and she adored Benny Goodman's music. She liked going to movies twice a week, thought *Romeo and Juliet* was the best picture she'd seen, and could eat chow mein a few times a week, too. She was afraid of fire. The closest friends to the Wills were Chick and Joan Chandler, Dr. Donovan Johnson (who delivered Beverly), and Ray and Mrs. McCarey.

In 1945 she told of another hobby: she crocheted the room-length white carpet herself for the guestroom. "It took all of my spare time for seven months. It grew so heavy that I had to sit on the floor with my crochet hook going like mad. Why did I do it? I wish I could tell you. But I had a kind of driving urge. The first time I looked at this room, I said to myself, 'What it needs is a white carpet.' And I didn't feel I could afford a really expensive one." She also made all the pillows on the davenport and upholstered all the furniture.

Filmed from mid-December to mid-January 1936, the 75-minute *Time Out for Romance* wasn't released until more than a year later on March 19, 1937. Based on the short story "Thanks for the Ride" by Eleanore Griffin and William Rankin, as published in *McCall's* magazine (November 1936), Malcolm St. Clair was originally set to direct, but fell ill and Fox's champ Allan Dwan stepped in to captain the screwball road picture.

Manipulative mother Vera Blanchard (Georgia Caine) has bribed Count Michael Montaine (Vernon Steele) to marry his daughter Barbara (Claire Trevor) in order to give the family a title. But when her father, tycoon James Blanchard (Andrew Tombes), learns of the plot, he informs her daughter by telegraph, causing her to lamb out and hitch a ride with Bob Reynolds (Michael Whalen). Bob is driving his new car to the West Coast as part of a caravan for boss Willoughby Sproggs (William Demarest), who would fire him for picking someone up on the road. The reluctant Bob complies, hiding Barbara when he can, but when she's finally discovered, she claimed to be Bob's wife whom he's deserting, so Willoughby forces Bob to bring her along. Things are further complicated when jewel thieves hide a diamond necklace in Bob's car, but it's a crap game that lands Barbara in jail, though Bob helps her escape. Followed by his caravan friends, everyone ends up in the slammer when Bob and Barbara are caught. Mr. Blanchard hurries out to spring his daughter, but after realizing the two are in love, he leaves them in the hoosegow embracing as he goes out to get an annulment from the Count.

Joan and Chick Chandler in *Time Out for Romance*, 1937.

Joan was Midge Dooley, a member of the caravan, and again *The New York Times* singled her out, caring more for Joan than the rest of the film. "Thanks to the presence of that spidery-legged comedienne Joan Davis, who is in the habit of knocking herself out as a form of protest against her human limitations, in one of the forward cars, the film may be classified as endurable second rate." *New York Daily News* was of exactly the same opinion: "Joan Davis is perfectly natural, her breezy brand of comedy gives the picture its chief reason for being noticed. Miss Davis is a comedienne to watch. She and her teammate, Chick Chandler, are the inspirations for most of the laughs heard at the Palace this week."

No wonder Joan made so many movies in 1937. She wasn't in them for very long. The best case in point is *Wake Up and Live*, the Ben Bernie/Walter Winchell feud musical in which Jack Haley becomes the biggest thing in radio as The Phantom Troubadour. Joan is on the screen for perhaps two minutes near the end, credited as "Spanish Dancer," giving a wild and sliding mime to music as she trips, falls, slips and cough-smokes her way around the polished dance floor.

Joan stole the show in *Wake Up and Live*, 1937.

Los Angeles Evening Herald Express (April 10, 1937) was wildly enthusiastic over this one, not just singling out Joan as "terrific in a comedy hit," but shouted that "*Wake Up and Live* has the spirited sparkle to make you do just that! It is the gayest, the zippiest of the current crop of tunefilms. It is more than that. It is entertainment plus! I've seen a great many musical films, but seldom have I been so thrilled, so much on the edge of the theater seat. Darryl Zanuck well earns another pat on the back as do all those concerned for this piece of top-notch entertainment." Jack Haley was repeatedly knighted as the movie's shining star, though his fine singing voice came from dubber Buddy Clark. *The Los Angeles Illustrated News* reveled in the Winchell/Bernie feud: "Down the valley of wisecracks, firing a steady barrage of insults at one another as they go, ride Walter Winchell and Ben Bernie." And, of course, "Joan Davis is outstanding in a burlesque Spanish fandango."

Sing and Be Happy (1937) was another Fox musical, this time with catchy tunes from Sidney Clare and Harry Akst, sung by Tony Martin and Leah Ray. Joan's role was small for third billing, but dueting with Chick Chandler on a song called "Pickles" can't make one complain much, and already showed her drawing power with Fox.

Sing and Be Happy, **1937.**

Buzz Mason (Tony Martin) doesn't want to give up crooning and his band for the life of an advertising man, but there's not much hope after he and the fellas cause $3,000 in traffic accidents in a small town by broadcasting from an airplane over a loudspeaker. His father John Mason (Berton Churchill) and Thomas Lane (Andrew Tombes) are competing for an advertising account, the latter using his daughter Ann (Leah Ray), to help him design sketches to wow the client. Buzz and Ann have been friends for years, but she doesn't take him seriously as a potential lover since he's always clowning. She begins to date co-worker Allan Howard (Allan Lane), and things get worse when Ann thinks Buzz has sabotaged her work for the ad campaign. He has a chance to prove himself when two daffy, singing window cleaners (Joan Davis and Chick Chandler) slip Buzz the knowledge that his father is trying to spike her chances at a singing audition for the client. Buzz foils his father's scheme, instead, punches Allan in the nose, and takes Ann away. The client is pleased with the window cleaners' ad song, "Pickles," but not so pleased when the contract she offers them is to clean the windows on the other side of the building.

If she wasn't getting plum parts, certainly Joan Davis was at least the girl to watch. Usually to watch fall down. Of her tolerance for posterior punishment, she told the press, "I've been very lucky in comedy falls all my life, with the exception of one that wasn't in the script for *Sing and Be Happy*. In that, I am a window washer—a rather sloppy one—and while walking with a pail of sudsy water in my hand, both feet skidded out from under me and it seemed like I hit the ceiling, only it was my back that suffered. I went to the hospital for eight days."

In 1938, after filming *My Lucky Star*, she explained to a newspaper just how to take a fall. "Having experienced some 20,000 impacts with floors of varying viscosity, I have at last thought up a bruiseless method of falling. In simple terms it is this: most people fall too suddenly and too hard. As Aristophanes (or somebody) once said, the greatest enjoyment of any pleasure comes from savoring it slowly. It is the same with falling. As soon as you trip, stop and think. Say to yourself, 'I am in no hurry. I must be cool and deliberate. I must keep my head down, my eyes on the wall and swing from the hips.' This is the delayed action, or perambulating method, and is recommended north of the Tropic of Capricorn. Do I make myself clear? Disaster awaits those who defy this principle. The boys in Sonja Henie's skating chorus experienced a rude awakening when they failed to apply my advice in early rehearsals on the huge ski slide. You should have seen them go flying around those hairpin turns at forty miles an hour! When they hit bottom, all my old scars began to throb in sympathy.

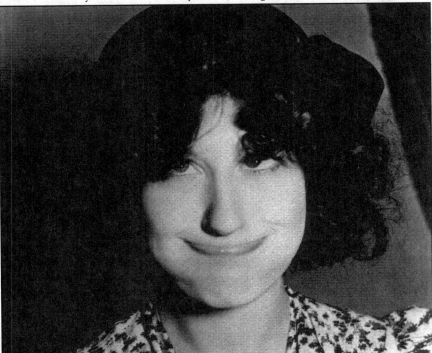

Playing for laughs in an early photo session.

"This brings me to the second phase, the 'juste milieu' or gentle touch. This is the matter of stroke. As you near the floor, you should reduce your speed so that, about 10 inches away from your destination, you are just gliding. The law of gravity, they tell me, says your speed always increases as you fall, but you can ignore this just as you can any other silly law.

"During the rehearsals for *My Lucky Star*, I imparted much of the foregoing information to Roy Del Ruth, who directed the picture. But directors are hard to impress. He just sat there and said there wouldn't be any falls in any of the big ice ballet scenes, thus dismissing entirely a discovery as important as that of the innerspring mattress.

"Speaking of mattresses, some people say it's nice to reach for a pillow as you fall. All I can say is, you'd have to have the services of both a valet and a prophet. But with my system, you can now walk—walk in the dark unscathed (much)—afraid no longer of the kid's toys, your wife's broom, or furniture on wheels. Me—I always carry a flashlight—I like to see where I'm falling!

"Well, you can try it on your own floor sometimes, but take out some good insurance first."

With Jane Withers in *Angel's Holiday*, 1937.

Filmed in a month between mid-February and mid-March, Fox's *Angel's Holiday* (1937) sidekicks Joan as Stivers, companion to screen star Pauline Kaye (Sally Blane) who is followed by June "Angel" Everett (little Jane Withers) in a farcical kidnapping plot that weaves much romance and high energy into a mere 74 minutes.

One of the more puzzling Joan Davis credits is for Fox's 1937 musical, *You Can't Have Everything*, starring Alice Faye, the Ritz Brothers and Don Ameche. It's been rumored that Joan appears in the film, and indeed the *Hollywood Reporter* listed her in the cast, but it's doubtful that she made it into the final cut of the picture. It wouldn't be the last time.

In fact, Fox began developing a script called *Song of the Islands* around this time for Faye, the Ritzes, Ameche and Davis, with various versions being reworked for Faye well into 1940, but ultimately the musical was released in 1942 with Betty Grable, Victor Mature and Jack Oakie in the leads.

Joan was also cast in one of Grable's best color musicals, *Moon Over Miami*, in 1941, but never appeared in the picture. Perhaps she was meant to take over the man-hungry Charlotte Greenwood role, always seeking wooden-faced Jack Haley—it's hard to say.

Hollywood was/is full of recasting decisions.

She was set to be in the Oscar-winning Fred Astaire-Ginger Rogers musical *Swing Time* (1936), but did she end up on the cutting room floor? She was cast and probably cut out of RKO's *Higher and Higher* (1943), the film version of the Rodgers & Hart musical, starring Jack Haley, Michele Morgan, and Frank Sinatra, which introduced the Jimmy McHugh-Harold Adamson standard "I Couldn't Sleep a Wink Last Night." Joan and many of the rest of the cast of Sun Valley Serenade were set to appear in its sequel, *Iceland* (1942), but only Sonja Henie made it back after the "sequel" idea was scratched. The Fox hillbilly story, *Kentucky Moonshine* (1938), that ultimately went to the Ritz Brothers, was originally conceived for Joan, Wally Vernon and Jack Haley. She was slated for Universal's *Private Buckaroo* (1942), but never joined The Andrews Sisters, Dick Foran and Joe E. Lewis in all that boogie.

Joan did have an interesting cameo as herself in Jane Withers' *Keep Smiling* (1938), about a little girl who goes to Hollywood to reform her drunken uncle, a director. Thankfully, Fox had longer-than-cameo plans for Ms. Davis.

Chapter 3
A Film Career

The Great Hospital Mystery (1937), based on the short story "Dead Yesterday" by Mignon G. Eberhart, which appeared in Pictorial Review (September 1936), gave Joan her first significant Fox role. As nurse Flossie Duffy, her scenes were mostly limited to non-plot comedy relief, though. She works under hospital supervisor Miss Keats (Jane Darwell), who seems to be the real detective of the mystery of the death of Allen Tracy (George Walcott) who visits his morgue intern friend Tom Kirby (Howard Phillips) in order to fake his death to escape bank robbers. When the charity case patient (thought to be Tracy) is found with a gunshot wound, the cops are on the scene, followed by the murder of Kirby. All is explained and the murderer is revealed to be . . . the cranky patient Flossie has had so much trouble with . . .

A killer, but not the killer, role in *The Great Hospital Mystery*, 1937.

According to *Variety*, Joan was the best part of the film. "Sole relief from the picture's dullness is provided by Joan Davis, who does her round-heeled slide juggling a bed pan and never spilling a drop." Under its alternate title, ***Dead Yesterday***, the 60-minute film was shot in less than a month in January of 1937 and released on May 14.

Filmed from September 13, 1937 through early November and released on the last day of that year, ***Love and Hisses*** did not afford Joan a lot of screen time, but the Simone Simon musical did give her one standout song, "Oh, What a Man," which she sang to pictures of her "hunk of stuff" Bert Lahr that are almost psychotically placed all around her room. As secretary to the great Walter Winchell (playing himself), Joan (known only as Joan) and Sugar Boles (Lahr), who works for Winchell's rival Ben Bernie (playing himself), go to great pains (literally) to keep their intense, dually-obsessive love affair a secret, one of them hiding in a closet or the bathroom whenever they are discovered in a passionate embrace.

(One of the gorilla-like embraces between Joan and Bert had to be shot again after a strap broke and Joan's slip fell to the floor. And in one newspaper it was reported that songwriter Sidney Mitchell tore the ligaments in his ankle on November 4, 1937 while trying to show Joan how to do falls to the rhythm of his song, "What a Man.")

Joan has nothing to do with the main plot which (once again) concerns the rivalry between Ben Bernie (also playing himself), who wants to make a star out of Yvette Guerin (Simon), and Winchell, who would rather not be told who should be a star. So Bernie decides to put one over on the great newspaper columnist by having him think he discovered this girl under a different name.

What a pair, what a pair! *Love and Hisses*, 1937.

Along the way the tables are turned when Winchell reeks his revenge with some gangster friends who kidnap Bernie and "Yvette Yvette," as she's now been christened by Winchell. Meantime, she's fallen for the hot-tempered songwriter (Dick Baldwin), whose songs she sings. Most of the catchy ditties were written by Fox stalwarts Mack Gordon and Harry Revel, though Joan's specialty number was penned by Lew Pollack and Sidney Mitchell.

Variety rightly growled that Joan "has only her gawks and grimaces to abet her; her lines are lean as bamboo sprouts." Still, as she told an interviewer on the set, "Even with 'hokum' comedy, which looks so natural, you need to study and study. One little slip of a finger, one slightly different expression on the face may make all the difference between getting a laugh or a shrug."

Thin Ice (1937) is a fairy tale for skater Lili Heiser (Sonja Henie) in St. Christophe, snuggly hidden in the Alps. It is there in that pristine village that she meets her Prince Rudolph (Tyrone Power), who introduces himself as a lowly newspaper reporter. Headlines of the two's romance mount higher and higher amid political in-fighting in the Prince's country, until finally the Prince knows the way to prove the stories are true is to marry the girl, whom he now loves. When Lili learns the truth from his lips, she faints dead away. But not too dead to awake in time for one last, big-budget skate.

Thin Ice (1937) may have been skating star Sonja Henie's vehicle, but, according to the ***Brooklyn Daily Eagle***, "the indescribably funny Joan Davis is at last given a major spot after a series of almost invisible support roles in Grade B flickers. Mere words do not quite catch the quality of Miss Davis' brand of humor. Superficially it is slapstick, but on second consideration it appears rather to be a super-sophisticated distillation of the most elegant type of humor. The comedienne goes directly to the heart of her material in an almost savage manner without once sacrificing method to mugging. You'll have to compare Miss Davis with the obvious Miss [Martha] Raye to see how good she is. Whatever closer analysis will reveal, there's no mistaking Miss Davis' presence in *Thin Ice*. Her songs are not in the front line of comic ditties, but she turns them into howlers."

Hollywood Citizen News agreed that "some riotous song and dance funmaking is exhibited by Joan Davis." *The Los Angeles Examiner* wrote that "two musical numbers are put over with a bang by Joan Davis, who seems to have been inserted into the picture for laughs—and she gets them. The lady is a wow, as witness her antics in 'I'm Olga from the Volga.'" They reported that the film itself was a crowd pleaser, especially due to its star. "If Shirley Temple were about ten years older, she'd have good cause to be jealous of the next-cutest thing in pictures, Sonja Henie, who returned with her second smash screen hit, *Thin Ice*, to be almost cooed over by the audiences at Grauman's Chinese and Loew's State theaters yesterday [September 1, 1937]."

The film's title had been changed from *Thin Ice* to *Lovely to Look At*, then back to *Thin Ice*, and was based on the play ***Der Komet*** (1922) by Attila Orbok. Adapted by Fanny and Frederic Hatton, the play opened in New York on October 23, 1930 as ***His Majesty's Car*** and starred Miriam Hopkins. This was Henie's second film, the petite charmer already sliding into the top ten moneymakers' list of 1937. Joan was credited as merely the "orchestra leader," but she still did the improbable with her musical numbers: she stole the show.

After scoring big in *Thin Ice*, the *Hollywood Citizen News* reported on September 3, 1937 that "Miss Davis has been signed to a term contract, and bigger and better assignments are in store for her." Louella O. Parsons' column in the *Los Angeles Examiner* a week later wrote that "Joan Davis danced on her heels in *Wake Up and Live*, and was immediately recognized as a potential movie favorite. But it really wasn't until she sang in *Thin Ice* that the Twentieth Century-Fox executives sat up and took notice. Here, right under their very noses, was a girl with that elusive something that leads to stardom. So it was up to the studio chieftains to find her a story.

"Well, that stellar crown will be placed on the Davis gal's head in *Kentucky Moonshine* as soon as she finishes *Sally, Irene and Mary*. She gets the top spot in this, a hillbilly musical which is being tailored to her measure."

With her newfound success, the *Los Angeles Examiner* printed a "Keyhole Portrait" on Joan in their day-after-Christmas 1937 edition. It gave a brief history of her life, and some interesting tidbits: ". . . years ago she started a file of gags and situations and has more than a dozen volumes . . . goes to the movies at least twice a week . . . bowls, swims, and golfs . . . was known as 'The Human Deer' in her school days . . . recently bet Disney animator Evelyn Parsons $50 she could outrun her in a 100-yard dash . . . although 17 pounds heavier, she beat former track star Parsons by two and a half yards; now she's looking for a bowling champ to mop up . . . she averages nine hours sleep, but can do 13 or 14 without effort . . . favorite perfume is Toujours Moi; favorite flower, the peony; color, cerise; things, *The Last Mile* was the best stage play she ever saw, and *Romeo and Juliet* the best picture . . . studied the violin as a child, and at the end of two years could play one piece, 'Pop Goes the Weasel.'"

The Ritz Brothers gave it that ol' college try in their own *Horse Feathers*-themed film, *Life Begins in College* (1937), and the results were typically hilarious for Fox. It was their most physical picture, and that's what the boys did best.

They play Klassy Kampus Kleaners who get mixed up in Lombardy College's football team by cleaning the trousers of American Indian quarterback George Black (somewhat similar to the great Jim Thorpe, played here by Nat Pendleton). Of course, the Ritz Brothers win the day with some creative football playing (making the other side commit penalties), with Harry Ritz catching his own pass to score the big game's final touchdown. Inez (Joan Davis) has had the hots for George all through the picture, and had a tattoo of a snake put on her arm (the only thing the big lug said will make him marry her), but after a barbarous kiss from him after the game, the poor girl tries to rub the tattoo off.

Filmed between July 12 and early September 1937, the original titles for the film included *Pigskin Parade of 1937*, *Pigskin Parade of 1938* and *1937 Pigskin Parade*. (Titles that were designed to cash-in on Fox's popular *Pigskin Parade*, released the previous year.) It was the Ritz Brothers' first starring feature film, opening in New York on September 24, 1937.

Love that Pendleton lug!

Los Angeles Evening Herald Express was crazy about the brothers, calling them "nothing short of a triple riot," while the film itself "is decidedly a deluge of daffiness." Parsons at the *Los Angeles Examiner* always had her eye out for Joan. This time "Davis doesn't have a very big role as the co-ed who is out to capture Nat's heart—but she makes every moment count, and her songs and dances are hilarious." And admits that, "fundamentally, the picture is built completely around the Ritzes, and they more than prove their ability to carry a production on their own."

On October 22, 1937, Joan made headlines in the *Los Angeles Examiner* when former Olympic star Olive Hatch sued her friend for $13,375 in Los Angeles Superior Court, claiming breech of contract. It seems Joan had entered into a contract with the swimming star to use her as her film agent, but "Joan refused to pay commissions on salaries already earned" and "also refused to accept other film work." Through her attorney Murray Riskin, Hatch asked for and received the total commissions she would have received at that point in the contract. With the end of that friendship, Joan became more careful with mixing relationships and money.

Sally, Irene and Mary (1938) was suggested by Edward Dowling and Cyrus Wood's 1922 play. Stars Alice Faye and Tony Martin were married a month before production began, but Fox studio head Darryl Zanuck gave the couple a wedding present of a trip to Europe after filming was completed. Filmed between November 8 and late December of 1937, the musical had its New York release on February 25 the following year.

Sally Day (Alice Faye), Irene Keene (Joan Davis) and Mary Stevens (Marjorie Weaver) trade in their jobs as manicurists in a barbershop to become cigarette and hatcheck girls at the Covered Wagon Café in Greenwich Village, where Sally meets singer Tommy Reynolds (Tony Martin). As the two fall in love, rival Joyce Taylor (Louise Hovick, a.k.a. Gypsy Rose Lee) puts up the loot to finance a Broadway show, having married and divorced seven millionaires, to star Sally, Irene, Mary and Tommy. When she sees Sally and Tommy kiss, the show's off. Luckily, Mary has inherited a steamship line, consisting of a lone, crappy tramp-steamer, so the gang decide to put on a floating show. Tommy doesn't want the dream to die for the kids, so agrees to marry Joyce in order to renovate the ship, and the show opens to big crowds. Irene tries to put one over on Joyce by having a real judge perform the marriage ceremony scene, but when he jumps ship due to the ship's boiler nearly exploding, the ship's captain steps in to save the day. Joyce goes for Baron Zorka (Gregory Ratoff), Irene goes for streetsweeper Jefferson Twitchell (Jimmy Durante), and the hit show just might go on forever.

Reviewing the film for *Hollywood Citizen News Radio*, Zuma Palmer wrote, "I thought Joan Davis as Irene rather stole the show when I saw it at the 20th Century-Fox studios." And Louella O. Parsons heralded for the *Los Angeles Examiner*: "The 1938 model of *Sally, Irene and Mary* has been completely renovated by Darryl Zanuck with new songs, gay romantic adventures and up to the minute comedy. While little of the original Broadway success other than a few stray tunes and the three girls in search of fame on Broadway, I know you will agree with me that the changes enhance rather than hurt the original play." She also called Joan "amusing" and her one number a "show stopper."

Joan was next up for the role of Libby Long (ultimately played by Inez Courtney) in *Five of a Kind* (1938), which turned out to be the third and final feature starring the Dionne Quintuplets. Again, it would have been a nothing part for Joan, but it was an interesting farce between battling radio broadcasters to see who would end up with the famed five on their show.

Hold That Co-Ed (1938) stars George Murphy as Rusty Stevens, one-time all-American for Clayton University, and John Barrymore, as Governor Gabby Harrigan, who is running for the US Senate. Hired to coach at State College, Rusty learns that the sports equipment budget has been chopped, so he organizes a student protest that gets them in trouble with the cops. The episode becomes a political pawn for power between Harrigan and the meek Republican candidate, Major Hubert Brekenridge (George Barbier). Harrigan's secretary, Marjorie Blake (Marjorie Weaver), who has become enamored of Rusty, pitches the grand idea of a Gabby Bowl stadium that could hold 100,000 people. The politician can't resist, but in the opening game, Harrigan is whacked in the head by Lizzie

ALL THESE STARS!
ALL THESE LAUGHS!
and Oh-h-h so much romance!

It's your top-hit musical (but TOP!)...with all the zing and extra sparkle you expect *and get* in a Darryl F. Zanuck show!

ALICE
FAYE · **MARTIN**
TONY

in

SALLY, IRENE *and* MARY

Three sirens of swing in search of Social Security!

A 20th Century-Fox Picture with

JIMMY DURANTE
GREGORY RATOFF
JOAN DAVIS
MARJORIE WEAVER
LOUISE HOVICK
J. EDWARD BROMBERG
BARNETT PARKER
AND
the leading comedian of screen and radio
FRED ALLEN

Directed by William A. Seiter
Associate Producer Gene Markey
Screen Play by Harry Tugend and Jack Yellen
Original Story by Karl Tunberg and Don
Ettinger · Suggested by the stage play by
Edward Dowling and Cyrus Wood

and
ALL THESE SONGS!
"Half Moon On The Hudson"
"I Could Use A Dream"
by Bullock and Spina
"Got My Mind On Music"
"Sweet As A Song"
by Gordon and Revel
and four more!

20th
CENTURY
FOX

Darryl F. Zanuck
In Charge of Production

Olsen's (Joan Davis) powerful kick. Daughter of a famous football coach, Lizzie is then let on the team for publicity reasons, being the sport's first female player. When she turns out to be too good (kicking the tying point in the first game), Harrigan decides to lace his team with professionals and soon bets Breckenridge the election: if State loses, he'll withdraw; if Clayton loses, Breckenridge must concede. It's all up to Lizzie. And the wind. It's fierce on that decisive day, blocking her kick and giving her hell on the last play of the game. But she's got gumption and finally, heroically falls over into the end zone, with a little encouragement from boyfriend Wilbur (Jack Haley), Harrigan's assistant.

George Murphy, Joan and the fellas of *Hold That Co-ed*, 1938.

During the filming of one 98-degree scene in the football stadium, it was reported that Joan collapsed from sun shock and was sent home. It wasn't her first accident on the very physical picture: after one particular fall, she had to have her arm in a brace beneath her woolen jersey.

Jimmy Starr for ***The Los Angeles Herald Evening Express*** wrote, "Because some folks doubted that Joan Davis actually did the goal kicking in *Hold That Co-Ed*, the comedienne has issued a challenge to any and all gals between the halves of our local football contests." The same paper wrote a week later that the picture was "filled with football thrills, rah-rah, tunes and political laughs from start to finish, it's a picture to send you out of the theater convinced that the movies are our best national tonic." And "if *Hold That Co-Ed*, with John Barrymore and Joan Davis, isn't the funniest picture of the year—it will do until something more hilarious comes along. Joan Davis has never been so funny. In fact, the hilarious highlight of the picture comes at the end when Joan attempts to score a touchdown against a headwind. Twice across the goal line, she is blown back, only to have to struggle to touchdown the ball once more. That she is also losing her football panties at the same time doesn't sadden the situation, either."

Upon seeing her in *Hold That Co-Ed*, playwright Kyle Crichton (author of ***The Happiest Millionaire***) wrote for *Collier's*, "She takes off into space in an array of limbs and arms resembling nothing other than an octopus taking a flying test, she ends by falling on her caboose with a crash that not only shakes the stadium but shakes the inherent faith of man in the frailty of woman." *Variety* thought that "Miss Davis is a near panic all the way, either on or off the football field and her presence, plus that of Barrymore, saves the picture." And ***Motion Picture Herald*** reported that they didn't "believe a picture has had our patrons howling like this one did at the close of the story. The second night we took a point of observation and it was a treat to see them eat up that slapstick finish. The picture pleased generally and did extra business."

Joan really runs with the ball in *Hold That Co-Ed*, 1938.

Filmed under the alternate title *Jo and Josette*, from late December 1937 through the middle of January 1938, Fox's *Josette* (1938) set brothers David Brossard, Jr. (Don Ameche) and Pierre Brossard (Robert Young) against each other for the affections of petite French singer Renee Le Blanc (Simone Simon), who pretends that she's Josette (Tala Birell) to find her big break singing at the Silver Moon Café in New Orleans. The Brossards try to buy her off, thinking she's the real Josette who has her gold-digging claws in their rich pop's fortune, but they start to fall for her themselves, causing a rivalry between them.

Joan sits in the back of this film again, this time as Simone's companion/maid, May Morris, catching the eye and quips of café owner Barney Barnaby (Bert Lahr). *Love and Hisses* proved Davis and Lahr made good comic, sometimes blessed, relief. *Josette* only proves the proof.

During filming, Joan announced to the press that she was considering a career as a director of film comedies, and had already taken up the study of film cutting (editing films was often the first step for a director). She rightly considered herself well-qualified to edit or instruct in the art of slapstick. "It may be a year or two before I attempt a directorial job, but I certainly intend to make the attempt. There is still plenty of room for those rib-tickling two-reelers." Unfortunately, nothing came of her desire.

Just Around the Corner (1938) also gave Joan high billing, but little else, in this Shirley Temple-filled comedy with songs.

With Shirley Temple in *Just Around the Corner*, 1938.

After seeing a preview, *Film Daily* wrote, "The latest of the Shirley Temple pictures is a grand piece of entertainment with a load of laughter. Joan Davis' appearance is too short, but the song and dance she does with Shirley is done very well."

Around this time (November 1938) one newspaper reported that five-year-old Beverly Wills was cast as Irene Dunne's daughter in *Love Affair* (1939). "The kid does perfect imitations of Joan's comedy falls. That is, they're usually perfect. The other day, she tripped in the middle of one at RKO and hit her head against the corner of a piano. Was knocked cold, but, after being revived, gamely carried on."

By age five, Beverly was already encouraged to be a ham. She would recite for any strangers who came to the house:

MY NAME IS BEVERLY WILLS
AND I LIVE IN BEVERLY HILLS.
MY MOTHER'S JOAN AND MY FATHER'S SI.
MOM'S AN ACTRESS AND SO AM I.

The proud parents had come to the uneasy realization that young Beverly was growing up just as awkward as her mom. Joan said at the time, "How the heck are we going to tell her? She's too young to understand she's funniest when she's most serious. I think we'll wait two years. If I could take it at seven, Beverly can."

Newspapers ran a cute story about her 10th birthday: all kids invited to her party had to buy a 25-cent war stamp before getting in. As of 1945, 12-year-old Beverly was attending school at a convent in Flintridge, near Pasadena. On Friday nights Si would drive her back home for the weekend where she would stay until Sunday afternoon.

Chapter 4

Lucky Star?

Well, maybe she wasn't a movie star yet. Joan's roles rolled between near absenteeism to hefty-to-the-plot corkers, but the fluctuation was simply too inconsistent to appease fans.

With billing just below Sonja Henie and Richard Greene, Joan still wasn't very necessary to *My Lucky Star* (1938), but the Mack Gordon/Harry Revel musical was another hot-on-the-ice time for film audiences. The *Los Angeles Herald Evening Express* thought the Alice in Wonderland ballet was the finest thing Henie had yet done on screen, and merely commented that "Joan Davis is amusing as Sonja's roommate."

With Buddy Ebsen in *My Lucky Star*, 1938.

Unfortunately, this was the film that cured Joan of clowning for a while. While rehearsing with Buddy Ebsen for a *Lucky Star* scene, she injured her back and, under doctor's orders, it kept her out of the pratfall game until *Sailor's Lady*, two years later. "I guess I didn't know my own strength, because, as Buddy gave a heave, I braced myself. We ended in a heap, with Buddy on top. He weighs a lot more than I, and the result was somewhat painful for me."

Joan's 1939 movie year began with *Tail Spin*, shot for Fox from September 24 to early December of the previous year. The film follows Trixie Lee (Alice Faye) in her determined course to win the Women's Trans-Continental Air Race, with the help of partner Babe Dugan (Joan Davis). Overcoming obstacles such as no money and a wrecked plane, she still manages to give her main competition, Gerry Lester (Constance Bennett), a run for her money, even though Gerry has a superior, newer plane. They also compete for Navy flyer Tex Price (Kane Richmond), but upon seeing the death of her married friends, also pilots, Trixie decides to give up her man and stick to flying, scoring herself a lucrative sponsorship offer from Sunbeam Oil in Los Angeles at just the right time.

Hollywood Citizen News called it "an extraordinarily dull and spiritless film, stodgily written throughout, awkwardly dialogued, and positively remarkable for the absence of dramatic entertainment. Joan Davis and Wally Vernon provide comedy relief, but what *Tail Spin* really needs is a scenario." *Film Daily* disagreed, writing, "for the first time the femmes do the thrills in the aviation field for the screen, and they manage to make an entertaining job of it. Some neat pathos and very strong suspense and thrills are injected." The always money-conscious *Motion Picture Herald* reported on May 6, "Just average program at op allocation. Too many air pictures; people are fed up on them. Good musicals and outdoor pictures with action is what we need. Business below average." But on June 3 things were looking up: "We did a fair business on this picture that features women and airplanes. There is plenty of sob stuff and the pace could be a lot faster, but the picture did please some of our patrons, and that is something. Worth a date but not at top allocation prices."

Filmed from September 9 through October 14, 1939, *Day-Time Wife* was mostly Tyrone Power and Linda Darnell's marital strife-comedy, but Joan had a few gags to throw as Warren William's receptionist. The main plot follows Jane Norton's (Linda Darnell) turmoil at finding out if her husband Ken (Tyrone Power) is cheating on her with his secretary after only two years of marriage. The title comes from Jane's desire to secure employment as a secretary and find out just what black magic secretaries hold over their bosses.

The *Los Angeles Examiner* told its readers, "you will be royally entertained," and singled out Joan as "a standout in her bit role. Her stamp licking routine will set you howling."

Daughter Beverly was making the news too, such as this charming little story in the *Los Angeles Examiner* from October 4, 1939: "Joan Davis had the cast of Daytime Wife in stitches yesterday telling them about her 6-year-old daughter, Beverly, who has just entered the first grade. Seems that Beverly came home the other day and Miss Davis asked her how things had gone in school. 'I got a gold star today,' Beverly replied, proudly. 'That's wonderful, dear,' replied Miss Davis. 'How did you earn it?' 'For relaxing,' replied little Beverly. 'Every day we have a rest period and today I fell asleep.'"

Joan wasn't sleeping on the Fox lot. *Too Busy to Work* was shot completely in the month of August 1939 and was released on November 17. With a working

Not much to do in *Day-Time Wife*, 1939.

title of *The Little Theater*, the film was based on the Howard Lindsay-Bertrand Robinson play, *Your Uncle Dudley*.

Becoming mayor of Maryville means self-absorbed John Jones (Jed Prouty) has less time for wife Louise (Spring Byington) and his drugstore, which already has to compete with Wilbur Wentworth's (Andrew Tombes) store. Feeling neglected, Louise gives the household reigns to thick-witted cousin Lolly (Joan Davis), and takes the lead in a new play. Thinking that the money for the hospital fund is just prop money, Lolly helpfully puts it in the safe, and with just an hour to go before that cash has to be at the state capitol, a local safe cracker is let out of jail to do his stuff. With a sigh of relief, Jones promises never to run for mayor again.

The money was great—$50,000 a year—for what seemed like little work (in terms of screen time), but for Joan's ego, apprehensive seeds were already being sown to get out of this highly visible Fox contract and into meatier roles. As of 1939 she was already heading back to the stage (with Si) periodically, where she now commanded feature billing and attained more than a comedic cameo.

As seemingly always, *Variety* was there to cover her exploits, as this review of her April 14, 1939 performance in Indianapolis observes: "Miss Davis does her eccentric dance and chin-socking(when she reprimands herself for stuttering), familiar to film patrons, and sings a medley of songs which she introduced in pictures. She works hard in the show to overcome a bad cold. Wills doesn't trade on the reputation of his wife, but does all right for himself with a comedy crystal reading bit and as a feeder for Miss Davis."

Perhaps tiring of a cameo career.

The new act provoked new offers, including one for a tour of the United Kingdom, but she was still under the thumb of a film contract and it was hard enough to get away for local stage work. Besides, as she told reporters at the time, "I waited for them and now they'll have to wait for me."

Later in 1939 she received featured press for another role: when 21-year-old sailor Richard H. Gray's car sideswiped another vehicle. Unfortunately, Joan and her friend Virginia White were his passengers. Gray informed the police that Joan advised him to drive away from the accident sight, a statement he later retracted, but not before making the headlines of most California newspapers.

Much of Joan's spare time was taken up with the public life that is necessary for a movie star; and she was eager for the bigger roles of a star. She attended movie premieres, such as for the Technicolor *Drums Along the Mohawk* in Fonda, New York, appearing with other Fox lot players Jane Withers, Lynn Bari and Eddie Collins.

Joan and husband Si were also making the rounds as a couple. They cut a rug at the 41 Club for singer Frances Faye's first night there, joining patrons John Wayne, John King, Phil Harris and other celebrities.

There were many slight news bits reported in the papers, true or not, to keep her comic image and name in the front of audiences' minds, to supplement some of her short stints on stage. On November 24, 1939, the *Los Angeles Examiner* wrote: "Joan Davis told this one at a personal appearance the other night. Seems she went riding with a handsome stranger and something 'awful happened. He parked the car, tried to kiss me and I slapped him.' 'What's so awful about that?' she was asked. 'Well, how did I know he chewed tobacco.'"

On January 29, 1940, the *Los Angeles Evening Herald Express* reported: "Joan Davis tells this swell kid story. The other night, her six-year-old daughter, Beverly, said, 'Mama, I stuck up for you at school today.'

"Joan asked her how that was.

"'Some of the kids,' explained Beverly, 'said you aren't as funny as you used to be.'

"'And what did you tell them?' asked Joan.

"'Well,' said Beverly, 'I told them you are not as young as you used to be.'"

When Joan signed with Fox in January 1940, on a yearly extension basis (she did not want a long-term contract, if she couldn't be sure of the size or type of her roles anymore), it was said, by some trade papers, that she was the only major female comedy talent under contract in Hollywood. It was a transitional time for comic queens: Judy Canova would sign with Republic later that year, and Paramount had severed their contract with Martha Raye, while Warner Bros. dropped the innocently sexy Marie Wilson. The fact that Joan had not gone overboard with screen time may have been the deciding factor in her longevity in a business where six months was a long time. Giving the audience just a little bit, sometimes in films where she was least expected, was apparently working in Joan's favor.

Her fan following was certainly evident in one article from the *Los Angeles Evening Herald Express*, which explained how a closeup of Linda Darnell in *Star Dust* had to be reshot after Fox looked at the rushes for the scene. There had been a large portrait of Joan doing one of her comic mugs behind her, and the brass was afraid the audience would be looking at her, undermining the dramatic scene.

Chapter 5
Physical

Keeping in shape for all the physical comedy wasn't easy. One press release stated that Joan suffered from numerous colds for which Si took her to see doctors and dieticians. She complained that she was always tired, the consensus of professional opinions being that she probably did not eat right during the long hours on the set. Raw fruits and vegetables were best, but before the days of

A sexy Joan Davis?

health-crazed America, it was difficult to attain anything greater than a portable machine to liquify fruits and veggies; and Joan didn't care for lumps in her liquid. Calling in an engineer, she and Si set to work to invent an early smoothie maker. Using a powerful motor (25,000 revolutions per minute), it broke down all cellulose and fibrous cells, not only completely liquifying vegetables and fruits, but meats or nuts as well. So, whenever Joan felt rundown on the set, she only needed to take a drink of beat or beef or carrot or pineapple to perk up with a well-balanced diet. It also gave Si something to do: marketing "The Hollywood Liquifier."

Apparently, Si even designed some of Joan's jewelry, including a pin which copied her signature.

Joan helped. In 1940 while on vacation at the Lone Palm Hotel in Palm Springs, she demonstrated the health marvel before a dozen guests. She liquified a whole cooked steak, drank half the juice herself and poured a little out for each guest. At the time, the Wills-owned factory making the machines, located at 4156 Beverly Blvd., was filling 200 orders a day. Si needed to expand to a larger location.

The comedienne needed the extra vitamins. It was tough looking after a 4-year-old daughter on the set and working at the same time. According to one report, this is exactly why Joan got Beverly into pictures in the first place—to give the little girl something to do! That same report stated that she made her film debut in Shirley Temple's *Rebecca of Sunnybrook Farm* (1938), but this is unlikely. It's written that Joan went to director Allan Dwan (himself a father, understanding the situation completely) and that he wrote in a sequence for Beverly in which she jammed a lollipop into Jack Haley's mouth "with comic vigor."

Joan said at the time, "The only time I think it's wrong for a mother to train a child towards an acting career is when the child shows a disinclination. I don't think any youngster should be forced into anything, she should merely be encouraged and assisted in whatever she shows most aptitude for and interest in."

Some nights, Joan would perform a little show for her daughter on the stage Si had built for working out their gags together (as they went over her scripts). Joan stated, "Playing for your own daughter is the most difficult assignment of all. She is more critical and doesn't mind in the least telling you what she thinks. I make sure, of course, before I start entertaining that she doesn't have any tomatoes or other small objects near her bed."

Filmed between December 13, 1939 and January 8, 1940 and released on March 29, *Free, Blonde and 21* was originally touted as the sequel to Fox's own *Elsa Maxwell's Hotel for Women*, with the working titles *The Girl from Kansas City* and *Hotel for Women No. 2*, but there was no connection to the earlier work.

It's a complicated plot originating at the Sherrington Hotel in New York City, where tenants Jerry Daily (Mary Beth Hughes) and Carol Northrup (Lynn Bari) become involved with doctors at the Mayberry Hospital after Jerry's failed

Gag shots for a magazine.

suicide attempt (the man she was seeing went back to his wife). Carol and Dr. Hugh's (Henry Wilcoxon) romance flourishes fine, but feeling ignored in favor of Dr. Stephen Greig's (Robert Lowery) job, Jerry starts seeing gangster Mickey Ryan (Alan Baxter), who is ultimately shot while killing someone. To help Jerry's "brother," as she calls him, Stephen comes to Hugh's beachhouse, where Mickey is holed up and dying; the young doctor tries but can't save him. Since it's his house, Hugh is implicated in covering up—and even murdering—Mickey, but Carol and Nellie (Joan Davis), the hotel maid, try to find evidence to the contrary. It's when Steven turns himself in, but keeps Jerry out of it, that the police trick Jerry into revealing that she's the one who's guilty, not Steven. Hugh and Carol are about to live happily ever after, but Nellie and boyfriend Gus (Chick Chandler), a cab driver, are still miles away from marriage.

Film Daily called this one a "moderately amusing comedy-melodrama . . . director Ricardo Cortze, who did a good job, depended on Joan Davis and Chick Chandler for the comic relief, but Miss Davis, alone, carries most of the comedy."

She had the waiting-around-the-studio time to carry more. Joan had been considered for the Tylette role in *The Blue Bird* (1940), which went instead to Gale Sondergaard. Based on a 1908 French play *L'Oiseau Blue* by Maurice Maeterlinck, the imaginative fantasy/fairy tale for children had Tylette (the family cat) and others seeking out the blue bird of happiness, which is eventually captured and flies away to freedom. It would have been a nicely alternative role for Joan's bio, but alas. She and singer Tony Martin were also planned to be a part of Fox's *Shooting High* (1940), another Hatfield/McCoy-type, star-crossed lovers musical-comedy.

Holding the line for an ample role.

In between roles, Joan coached old/young friend Jane Withers and Katharine Aldridge on how to fall down a 46-step staircase, which they accomplished in one take—a studio record, and which was expected to take a day and a half!—for 1940's *The Girl from Avenue A*.

Back to screen work.

Shot during a 30-day period in January and February 1940 and released on July 5th, *Sailor's Lady* once again pushed Joan Davis into a few sparse scenes, this time to support star Nancy Kelly. The real story involves Sally Gilroy (Kelly), sweetheart to sailor Danny Malone (Jon Hall), who has adopted a child, "Skipper," as a surprise to her finance. Though the child nets him a promotion, she also causes a fight at a party, bringing the shore patrol down on them, and

A wardrobe test for *Sailor's Lady*, 1940.

almost breaks Sally and Danny up. But she also secures Danny's Captain Roscoe (Charles D. Brown) a commondation—by stopping a gun practice which was upsetting the baby—and leads to Danny and Sally's marriage at the Church of Good Shepherd.

Fox's *Manhattan Heartbeat* was shot in just a few weeks in March and April of 1940. Based on the novel and play *Bad Girl* by Vina Delmar, this movie went through a few working titles, including *Rain or Shine* and *Marriage in Transit*.

Manhattan Heartbeat, 1940.

On their train back from a vacation at Camp Mohawk, Manhattan department store salesgirls Dottie Haley (Virginia Gilmore) and Edna Higgins (Joan Davis) meet up with Spike (Edmund MacDonald) and woman-hater Johnny Farrell (Robert Sterling). He's not against females enough to stay away from the store and chat Dottie up for a date. As the couple fall in love, Johnny saves up his bucks to buy the airport owned by his boss. Ten weeks after their marriage Dottie finds that she's pregnant, and she's scared to death because of his finances and the fact that her mother died in childbirth. She doesn't tell her husband of the child and her melancholy attitude makes him think she wants nicer things out of life, so he splurges his airport money on a fine apartment. Edna finally blurts the truth and Johnny is determined to provide Dottie with Bentley (Paul Harvey), the finest and most expensive doctor around. He even pilots a dangerous test flight to raise the money, but it's still not enough. When it's time, desperate Johnny races to Bentley's house and moves the good doctor with words of love for his wife. Not only does Bentley deliver a healthy baby boy, he pays the hospital bill and gives the tyke $50 to start a savings account. Only in the movies . . .

The *New York Daily News'* Kate Cameron commented that "Joan Davis, who can make an old gag look like something brand new in the comedy line, does her best to inject a light and lively tone to a depressing and twice-told film tale." *Film Daily* loved it at its Hollywood preview in June: "This considerably changed version of Vina Delmar's *Bad Girl* is an ideal vehicle for the talents of two screen newcomers, Robert Sterling and Virginia Gilmore. Joan Davis, of course, does outstanding work, garnering a heavy quota of laughs with her songs, antics and comedy. David Burton has supplied expert, sympathetic direction, blending the comedy, romantic and dramatic elements effectively."

During the filming of *Manhattan Heartbeat* it was reported that Joan was going on the road to promote husband Si's "new vegetable liquefier," making personal appearances at some of the bigger stores. But she never said no to a Fox part.

For Beauty's Sake (1941) was filmed in a fast 16 days on the Fox lot, based on Clarence Budington Kelland's 1939 novel *Skin Deep*. It tells the story of Bertram Erasmus Dillsome (Ted North), assistant astronomy professor, who is to inherit

Joan and Marjorie Weaver in *For Beauty's Sake*, 1941.

his aunt's estate if he can successfully manage her beauty salon for two years. With the aid of his girlfriend's (Marjorie Weaver) father's publicity man, Jonathan B. Sweet (Ned Sparks), they promote him as Dr. Erasmus, a French expert who knows the secret of eternal youth. The busy shop is soon immersed in lawsuits, murder and blackmail, but with the help of assistants Dottie Nickerson (Joan Davis) and Miss Sawter (Lenita Lane), the blackmailing ring that had been operating out of the salon (women love to tell secrets when having their hair dried) is foiled and all ends *beautifully*.

Reviewers were repeating themselves. As usual, *Variety* liked the comic relief more than the picture. "Joan Davis' comedy material, while somewhat questionable as far as gusty laughs are concerned, may be overlooked to some extent by the comedienne's innate ability. She's one of the cast's lone redeeming features."

A cut number from Sun Valley Serenade, 1941.

Joan was thoroughly underused in the hit Sonja Henie/John Payne musical *Sun Valley Serenade* (1941), though her three brief scenes were memorable comic foil for Milton Berle, who plays bandleader Glenn Miller's manager. She first meets him as he comes off the train to the winter resort, Sun Valley, but her next two scenes hurriedly make you watch the rest of the picture waiting for more Joan. When she collects a dime for charity from Berle and tells him that she has eighteen boyfriends, he slyly asks, "Eighteen? All told?" "No," she honestly answers, "one kept his mouth shut." When she meets him in the hall just a little while later, she forgot she'd already collected a dime from this mug, so quickly marks a large X on his shirt with chalk.

Joan did film a burlesque of *The Dying Swan*, a number that Sonja had made famous on the ice when she first became a professional skater. Originally intended for Henie's first picture, *One in a Million*, the number was scrapped in *Sun Valley* since both star and studio wanted something quicker and more spectacular, even though costumes had already been made.

A posed shot for *Sun Valley Serenade*, 1941.

The picture's Harry Warren/Mack Gordon score contained the classics "It Happened in Sun Valley" and "Chattanooga Choo Choo," the latter nominated for an Oscar. It also introduced Miller's signature tune, "In the Mood" to film audiences, but unfortunately Joan's one comic song, "I'm Lena, the Ballerina" was one of three unused songs written by Warren/Gordon and was the only one of the three to be shot. Apparently the PCA objected to part of the song's lyrics, which contributed to its being cut. The film, reportedly Henie's favorite role of her career, was also nominated for Best Cinematography and Best Music Scoring of a Musical Picture at the Academy Awards.

As *The New York Post* rightly wrote, "Joan Davis flits by the camera so fast that you hardly have time to identify her." *Film Daily*'s blurb, after seeing the Hollywood preview, was richly enthusiastic: "Outstanding entertainment is rich in laughs—drama and action is certain to hit the box office bull's eye." At an audience preview, *FD* continued the compliments, "Former reaction to pictures of this type—that there was too much spectacle and not enough story—will never be mentioned by those who see *Valley*. There is everything needed in this: laughs, action, drama, cute new twists and that superb Milton Berle humor. The skating scenes are lovely. Direction, superb. Photography, excellent."

Luckily there was a part with meat on it next. Produced in a mere two weeks in May of 1941, *Two Latins from Manhattan* (released on October 2) starred Joan as Joan Daley, publicity agent for New York's Silver Key nightclub, who substitutes her roommates, Jinx Terry (model Jinx Falkenburg) and Lois Morgan (Joan Woodbury), who happen to be aspiring singers, in place of the two Cubans she originally hired, but who were "hijacked" by a rival nightclub. Of course, the girls wow the audience and sign a lucrative contract, but soon the cat's out of the bag that these dames are really from Brooklyn, after the real singers return from

Cuba. But when Joan explains the situation to the audience, the people don't care! The happy audience is thrilled with the Americans, joining in on the conga line to dance out the story.

Two Latins from Manhattan (1941). L to R: Joan Woodbury, Jinx Falkenburg and JD.

Originally baptized *Girls from Panama*, Joan was borrowed from Fox for this Columbia picture, giving her top billing and an ample chance at that nervous comedy she knew so well. She did her best with average material. *Film Daily*'s headline ran: "So-So musical suffers from poor script and direction," and went on to complain that "it is rather difficult to predict with any degree of accuracy the possibilities of this picture, because while it is badly directed, and not too intelligently cast, there are other factors which some audiences will find pleasing and others possibly entertaining" which did include "the fake, forced comedy of the really talented Joan Davis" and "the over-involved situations, and the 'driven' attitude of most of the cast toward each other, the director, the script and, during particularly belligerent moments, toward the innocent, bystanding audience."

Chapter 6
Hungry Man Radio

The constant picture work was playing havoc with Joan's private life. Perhaps it was the long hours at the studio, and/or Si felt neglected as both husband and talent; perhaps Joan was achieving her goals outside her homelife; the only thing that's certain is that the Wills-Davis collaboration wasn't collaborating at home. In the early 1940s, the seeds of divorce were under the earth being rained upon. One unknown news source positively reported that "after only 10 days of their scheduled three months trial separation, Joan Davis, film comedienne, and her husband, Si Wills, have decided that they still love each other. The pair are back together again, Miss Davis revealed today, and are better off for the atmosphere having been cleared. 'The little vacation apparently was just what we needed,' explained the comedienne. 'It quickly proved to us that we didn't want to live apart.'" What it more than likely proved was that the studio machine didn't like adverse publicity. Divorce was inevitable.

Concerned that she was making too many pictures (and maybe, due to the strain it was putting on her marriage), Joan asked to be released from her 20th Century-Fox contract and began making the rounds as a freelancer in 1941. She said at the time, "In my heart, I feel I am so much more than a screwball." She also used the free hours to play in that popular medium, radio.

The main concern most of the industry had, Joan herself included, was if her style of zany comedy could adapt well to the medium of sound-only gags. No getting away with pratfalls, mugs and lanky leg tricks here. She didn't need them, anyway. Being an old trouper from vaudeville meant you had to be a master of many talents if you wanted to beat out the competition for paychecks and applause.

The Rudy Vallee Show was famed for its star's unfailing ability to find the best new acts. Joan wasn't new, but she was to radio. Vallee had discovered Frances Langford, and gave first big radio breaks to the likes of Beatrice Lillie, Milton Berle, Joe Penner and Edgar Bergen. Joan Davis got more than a big break; she eventually pretty much took over the crooner's show.

On one of her first radio performances, in the fall of 1941, she belted a version of "Hey Daddy," which soon lapsed into a comic monologue. *Variety* applauded the refreshing change. "It was a new idea and it was good—and so was she." It

Laying one on Vallee.

led to further radio bookings, especially on Vallee's Sealtest-sponsored series. And in August of 1942 she slipped into her most memorable radio series as a regular cast member at the rate of $1,500 a week.

Said *Radio Fanfare* on February 26, 1942: "Joan Davis has always been known as a very clever comedienne, but in radio her talents were confined to an occasional guest spot until she was invited to join the regular cast of *The Rudy Vallee Show*. She has proved a great asset to a very entertaining program. Her zany interpretations of popular songs and her marvelous flair for punching and timing good comedy lines have given America needed laughter. In tonight's show at 7, KECA, Joan plays an office secretary, with Robert Benchley cast as an ad agency head, Vallee as a radio contact man and John Barrymore as a sponsor."

"It was a privilege to work with John Barrymore," Joan told *Silver Screen* magazine in 1944. "He was literally dying then, but he was always a good trouper; he always gave a fine performance. During one show he fell sound asleep. I went over to awaken him. He was due at the mike. Quickly, he shuffled the cardboards in his hand [each page of his script was attached to cardboard backing] as though they were a pack of playing cards. He selected one at random and headed for the mike. It was the right one!

"He was a chain smoker. During one broadcast his cigarette went out. Absent-mindedly, he reached into his pocket, pulled out a big kitchen match and scratched it on the mike!

"Mr. Barrymore's last radio lines were said with me. It was a Tuesday preview and we were doing *Romeo and Juliet*. I have the recording now of his dramatic voice saying, 'What light through yon window breaks . . .'"

After the death of John Barrymore in 1942, Joan was invited by Vallee for two more guest appearances. Soon she was making an impressive $100,000 a year in radio. When Vallee enlisted in the Coast Guard in July of 1943, the star onus was thrust upon Joan, but sponsors were hesitant to trust her "novice" shoulders with all the responsibility. Jack Haley was brought in as straight man this time, which led to a reformatting of the series when *The Sealtest Village Store* began broadcasting its variety to audiences on July 8, 1943. As popularity of the series grew—and grow it did once audiences heard more of Joan—the sponsor had more confidence in their productive goldmine. Later in 1943 she turned down American Tobacco's offer of $15,000 a show when they wanted her to direct and produce the show as well; it was too much work, she said. Another report indicates that after Vallee's induction, Joan was offered $2,500 a week to be responsible for the entire show, and took it.

"I felt plenty scared," Joan said in a later interview, "but then I didn't realize how scared I'd be when Thursday night rolled around and X marked the spot, and the spot was me. I was so nervous that my lines were actually blurred at rehearsal. Then something happened which may happen to many people in charge of a business when they realize that they have others to think of besides themselves. Shortly I began thinking about the other members of the cast. Keeping on in this program meant something to them. I wasn't the only one. But the show wouldn't keep on unless we all pulled together. After that my nervousness was gone; I had reasoned myself out of it. Then I could buckle down to work.

"My formula is the girl who never gets her man, but never gets over trying to get him. I don't know why such a situation should be comic, but it seems to be. Perhaps because I keep up my courage in the face of many obstacles."

Whether it was a rehearsed ad-lib or not, one week, to perpetuate her man-hungry myth, when the script called for Rudy to kiss Joan, he started to make the usual hand-to-lips sound effect with his hand when she yelled, "None of that! I've waited over a year for this!" and smacked a kiss resoundingly on the blushing Vallee. The audience roared.

The studio audience was usually laughing louder than fans at home, at things that weren't even mentioned to those listening in. But Joan didn't care. A laugh was a laugh. "Radio work is much different from movie work. I think of radio as still being the theatre and forget the mike. Frankly, I mug and jump all over the place. Sure, I know that my bigger audience is listening in, but if I can act the way I do before a theatre audience I can do my stuff better so I can, in that way, give a better performance for the people at home—say, am I getting complicated or am I getting complicated?"

Joan had a hit on her hands, and she was finally the star. Entertainment historian James Robert Parish commented that "part of Joan's amazing radio success was due to her deep, well-modulated voice, which could transcend from a low screech to a high-pitched, cracking quiver in no time flat. The timber of her voice gave substance to her jokes and aided tremendously in her song renditions."

Her work on jokes and script punching-up encouraged Joan and Si to assemble a gag book. The Wills had a collection of more than 150,000 jokes, gags, routines and comedy material they had assembled since their vaudeville days, and the duo thought now was the time to seek a publisher. Within a week of assembling the material, they had a contract from one. Though the press reported that books were expected any day now, it's unclear why the project never happened.

As of 1945 Joan Davis would have the top comedy program on the air, her ratings shooting from 19.07 in 1944 to 26.0. Only Bob Hope and Fibber McGee & Molly were keeping her out of the #1 spot.

In 1944, sponsor Sealtest released a sweet & desperate promotional booklet entitled *The Life and Loves of Joan Davis*, supposedly written by the star herself. If *any* of it was written by Joan is impossible to say, and probably unlikely, but the comical publication gives daft insight into the *Village Store*, its portrayal of the perpetually single "Joan," and some prime examples of gags used on the show.

FOREWORD

For years now I have remained quiescent while vicious canards have been bruited about concerning my physiognomy. (Hey, did that language come outta me!) I have been accused of having bow legs, knock-knees, a skinny figure, a pointed head, a tapering nose, and of being unkind to my mother. All I can say is—"It's a lie!" I have always been kind to my mother. And so, in response to millions of requests (well, thousands, then. Hundreds? Anyway, I *know* I got a postcard), I have decided to write the true story of my life and loves, in odd moments here in the Sealtest Village Store. And, believe me, I have some odd moments.

JOAN DAVIS

THE LIFE AND LOVES OF JOAN DAVIS

I was born in Minnesota, where men were men and women know nothing about riveting. My family lived near the Twin Cities, but just before I was born, Dad had a premonition and moved away.

Dad used to tell me about those days. He said that he had always wanted a child. In fact, he'd have given anything if I'd been one. He told me that, when I was a baby, I looked exactly like him. Gee, I must have been a cute-looking kid with a diaper on one end and a toupee on the other.

When the nurse came to him in the hospital, she announced—"You are the father of a bouncing baby girl." And I was a bouncing baby. Gee, what fun they used to have dribbling me up and down the hall and scoring goals in the dining room chandelier with me.

Father rushed into the room to look at me—his first-born child. Then he rushed out and called his insurance company and said—"I want to report an accident."

Father was a baseball pitcher, and I, too, have always been interested in sports ever since I can remember. In fact, I was born with two strikes on me. When I grew a little older, they let me join Dad's team. No, I didn't play. They painted me white and used me for the left-field foul line.

Oh, darn it, I'll have to stop now.
Here comes a customer into the Sealtest Village Store.
Well, if it isn't the town's dumpiest dowager, Blossom Blimp [Verna Felton].

JOAN: Hiya, Blimpy, how's things?

BLOSSOM: Oh, hello, Miss Davis. I want something for my hands. Do you have any ointment?

JOAN: What kind of mint?

BLOSSOM: Oint—oint—oint.

JOAN: It ain't safe to go around talking like that with bacon so scarce.

BLOSSOM: Ah, Miss Davis, you're just jealous. Why, I'll have you to know that when I was a little younger, I was a famous actress. Why, three men were in love with me . . . Roger, Philip and Grant. When I refused them Roger took poison, Philip took gas . . .

JOAN: And Grant took Richmond.

BLOSSOM: Miss Davis, please. Ah, yes! Just thinking of
             my acting days makes me want to sing: Ahh!
             I was behind the footlights
             I acted on the stage
             I still can act most anything
             Except my age! WHOO . . . WOO. Goodbye.

Now, there goes a Blimp who really needs a ground crew to bring her down.
Oh, well—back to my life story.

Ah, but acting was always my real love. Even as a little girl I had quite a leaning towards the stage. As a matter of fact, I leaned towards the stage so much I kept falling out of the balcony.

My first appearance was in a beautiful tableau. I played the part of an angel with gossamer wings, but they fired me for going on maneuvers with a squadron of P-39's.

Then came my first singing role. What a triumph! The manager said I could sing for him till the cows came home; but as soon as they came home he threw me out.

Then another agent interviewed me. He wanted to know if I could play a character in a tragedy. So, I just told him that I was probably one of the most tragic characters he'd ever seen. That play was a survival of **Way Down East**. No, not a revival; this was a survival. We were lucky to live through the first act.

All this time I was studying music at the Conservatory. As my instructor used to say—"Why, when Joanie came to us, she didn't know a musical instrumental from a hole in the wall. And now, after only six months, she is the only girl in the whole world who can play a hole in the wall."

But the flute was my real love. Ah, when I played, how I put everything I had into that flute! And with my shape I could just make it.

Then came my big opportunity. I went on tour with an opera company. Why, when I opened in Frisco the house came down. Of course, they couldn't have those earthquakes every day.

Gee, what a great last act that opera had. There was a big quartet number sung by four Spanish noblemen—Don Giovanni, Don Giuseppi, Don Pasquale and Don By The Old Mill Stream. Then the opera ended with a big dueling scene. The baritone entered carrying a lance. Just as he started to throw the lance he was hit in the leg with four spears, and the curtain came down as he sang that famous aria—"I'm Lancing with Spears in My Thighs."

What a scene! What actors! But we didn't have a very long run. The audience chased us only three blocks.

Uh-oh, it's Thursday night and here comes Jack Haley—my new manager at the Sealtest Village Store.

HALEY: Hello, Joan. Anything happen in the Village this week?

JOAN: Yeah, Jack. My brother got drafted.

HALEY: Oh, I thought he had dependents.

JOAN: He did, but they took him anyway.

HALEY: Who was dependent upon him?

JOAN: Two bookmakers and a pinball machine.

HALEY: Well, there's a shortage of men, Joan.

JOAN: You're telling *me* about the man power shortage. Say, Jack, haven't you ever thought of getting married and settling down? Everyone should have a wife, you know.

HALEY: Oh, I don't know. My mother got along without one. But on second thought, a home and wife wouldn't be bad, and maybe in a couple of years the stork would come to our house.

JOAN: The stork! Gee, Jack, I can just picture the little one. He'll look like you.

HALEY: Yeah, and he'll have my brains. Why, some day he may grow up to be President.

JOAN: Yeah, just think—we'll have the only stork that ever became President.

HALEY: I'm talking about babies.

JOAN: Oh, babies! How many will we have, Jack?

HALEY: Aw, I'll let you keep score. Ah, Joanie, you've made me see things in a new light. How would you like to change your name?

JOAN: I'd love to.

HALEY: Well, why don't you try Schwartz? That's a nice name.

JOAN: Oh, Jack. You're turning me down again.

HALEY: Well, Joan, you know I'm *that way* about Penny Cartwright [Sharon Douglas].

JOAN:	Aw, what's she got that I couldn't have straightened and simonized?
HALEY:	Why, here she comes now. What effervescence! What sparkle!
PENNY:	Hello, everybody.
JOAN:	Hi-ya, Alka-Seltzer.
PENNY:	Oh, Jack, look what working in my garden did to my itty, bitty hands.
JOAN:	It didn't do your dweat big flat feet any good either.
HALEY:	Well, dear, you shouldn't try to do all the work yourself.
PENNY:	Oh, mother helps me. She uses an old rake that's been lying around the house for years.
JOAN:	That's *no* way to talk about your father.
PENNY:	Well, I have to go now. Goodbye.
HALEY:	Goodbye, precious.
JOAN:	Aw, precious.
HALEY:	Oh, don't worry, Joan. Do you know who's in town? DENNIS DAY!
JOAN:	You mean *the* DENNIS DAY from Jack Benny's program? Say, how about bringing him up to my house for dinner tonight?
HALEY:	Okay, that's a date. See you at the house.

Gee, DENNIS DAY coming for dinner. Boy, am I glad I went to that cooking school. I'll never forget that first day at cooking class. I spent the whole afternoon over a boiled rabbit—but I couldn't sober him up. Everybody says my cakes are heavy, but it isn't so. Sometimes I wonder, though, why I have the only bowlegged stove in town. Oh, well, back to my story.

After opera, I tried out for one of those high society dramas where you have to be decorous. The producer asked me what I knew about being decorous.

That was silly, because I had been in de-corus at Minsky's for three years.

Then came my big success as a seductive woman. They thought I couldn't play a vampire, but I told them off. I said, "Why, everybody says I'm bats."

Then Hollywood called me. The Chamber of Commerce claims they got a wrong number, but there I was in glamorous, exotic Hollywood. Ah, it was just one handsome man after another. If I couldn't get one, I'd go after another.

There was a continuous round of gaiety: Dinner parties, theatres, dancing. Why, one night at the Palladium I danced my head off; but somebody found it and turned it in at the Lost and Found.

Gee, how the men pursued me. One day I came out of a beauty parlor, and a fellow started chasing me. Finally he caught up to me and said, "Lady, I'm a lawyer. Tell me who did it and we can sue them for a million bucks."

The Hollywood Canteen asked for volunteers to entertain service men, and, naturally, I responded. I met a cute sergeant there one night, and did we hit it off together. I kept putting my head on his shoulder and he kept hitting it off. He was quick on the proposing, too. He told me that his heart said "yes," but his mind said, "no." He's going to call me up as soon as he hears from his liver.

But what a nerve that fresh corporal had saying that my legs looked like matchsticks. I guess I told him. They might look like sticks, but they don't match.

One night they announced that there was to be a beauty contest. I said, "Oh, boy . . . that's right up my alley." And, that's right where they hid me till the contest was over.

A captain drove me home one rainy night, and all the way home he kept asking me to marry him. But I lost him. He thought I was refusing him because I kept shaking my head. I tried to explain that my nose was caught in the windshield wiper.

Then I met an aviator at the Canteen. He took me up in his plane one day. He did some loops and spins, and then he asked me if I'd like to go into a dive. But, I told him he could take me to a nice place or none at all.

Hey, I better close up the store and go home. DENNIS DAY is coming for dinner.
❖ ❖ ❖ *(That means a lapse of time, and dinner's over.)*

DENNIS: Gee, that sure was a swell dinner, Miss Davis.

HALEY: It sure was, Joan.

JOAN: Why, thanks, fellows.

DENNIS: I can't understand why anybody as pretty as you isn't married, Miss Davis.

JOAN: Oh, brother! You hold him, Jack, and I'll run for the preacher.

HALEY: Easy, Joan. Would you like a cigarette, Dennis?

DENNIS: Oh, no, thanks. I never smoke on account of mother.

JOAN: Oh, does your mother say you're too young to smoke cigarettes?

DENNIS: Oh, no, she says I'm not old enough to light matches.

JOAN: Come over here and sit beside me, Dennis. Now, what would you like to do?

DENNIS: I'd like to look at your family album.

HALEY: This kid probably goes to a burlesque show just to listen to the music.

JOAN: Well, first I ought to tell you, Dennis, that I was a foundling. When I was a little baby somebody left me on a doorstep.

DENNIS: Gee, what happened?

JOAN: Some wise guy wrote "Welcome" on my chest and people kept wiping their feet on me till I was three years old.

DENNIS: Who's this on this page?

JOAN: That's my stout aunt—Aunt Matilda.

DENNIS: What's that in back of your Aunt Matilda?

JOAN: That's still Aunt Matilda. And over here is my rich uncle. You know, when I get married he's going to give me a dowry. He's got a lot of money and he is going to make

	it worthwhile for the man who marries me.
HALEY:	Oh, nobody's got that much money, Joan.
DENNIS:	Gee, all this talk about marriage. I just came up here for dinner. I don't want to get married. I'm going home.

❖　❖　❖

JOAN:	Ah, there he goes, DENNIS DAY—the only man I ever loved. But, I'll find a man someday, Jack.
HALEY:	I doubt it.
JOAN:	Oh, yeah! Why, just the other day I asked a handsome chap to get married. And, would you believe it—the very next day he married one of the nicest girls you'd ever want to meet.
HALEY:	The trouble with you, Joan, is you're not glamorous.
JOAN:	Who's not glamorous? After all, I'm almost as attractive as Hedy Lamarr or Veronica Lake. Why, just the other day I walked down the street with my hair combed over one eye. And, do you know what everybody said? They said, "There goes Joan Davis with her hair combed over one eye."
HALEY:	Aw, forget it, Joan. See you in the morning.

Well, here it is, another day at the Sealtest Village Store. Guess I'll write some more of my life story. Let's see, where did I leave off.

Ah, yes! Then came my big moment. I met Rudy Vallee. There he was seated across the room from me in a restaurant. I sent a waitress over to ask him to dance. He looked over, smiled at me, got up—and danced with the waitress. Then we went up to his house, where he showed me all his heirlooms. He had one piece that was priceless—an antique love seat. And, believe me, it came in handy with all of those antiques he makes love to.

While driving me home, he told me I had a face like the one that launched a thousand ships. I thought he meant Helen of Troy, but he said, "No—Henry Kaiser."

Ah, how suave and sophisticated he was. Why, a Duke visiting in Hollywood was so impressed that he asked Rudy to give him lessons in deportment. And Rudy did so well that in two weeks the guy was deported.

Rudy asked me what I thought of private schools. I told him that I didn't see any need for them as I'd been out with a lot of privates, and, brother, there's nothing left for them to learn.

It was Rudy, too, that suggested I go to a plastic surgeon and get my nose tilted upwards so I'd have that haughty air. But, I guess the doctor tilted it too far, because, now, every time I sneeze my hat blows off.

Gee, we had swell times. One day he took me to the beach. And, when I stood up and took off my robe the fellow next to me said, "Well, that's the first time I ever saw them unveil a mashie niblick."

I had one of those modern bathing suits on. You know—two bandanas and a prayer. I was swimming away out in the ocean when a shark came up alongside of me and said, "Hey, Bud, as soon as it gets a little darker what say if we swim in and get a couple of humans."

It was on our first trip to the beach that Rudy kissed me with fervor. He had a fervor of 104 and didn't know what he was doing.

Finally, Rudy asked me to work for him in the Sealtest Village Store. "Joan," he said, "you have a good head for figures. Now if you can only get a better figure for that head."

So, I took the job. After all, my family has always been prominent in business. Why, my Uncle came to this town barefoot thirty years ago. And, do you know what he wound up with? Very sore feet!

Gee, we had swell times together at the store. I did all the typing. It was kinda confusing at first, because every time I'd come to the end of a line a bell would ring and I'd go out to lunch.

We had the nicest class of people come in, too. One day that suave, sophisticated man-about-town, Bert Lahr came in. He was always crazy about me. Yes, the doorbell tinkled, and there he stood.

BERT:	Hello, Joan.
JOAN:	Ah, Bert. Rudy isn't here today. Isn't it wonderful?
BERT:	Yeah.

JOAN:	Gee, don't you love being alone?
BERT:	Yeah—why don't you beat it?
JOAN:	But, Bert, don't you see how deeply I care for you?
BERT:	Why, Joanie, would you throw yourself at me—a strange man?
JOAN:	Listen, I've thrown myself at stranger men than you.
BERT:	The trouble with you, Joan, is you're a member of the hoi-polloi.
JOAN:	So what? I'll resign. Look, Bert, we could get married.
BERT:	Married.
JOAN:	Yeah. Just think, if we were married, every time you came into the house, you'd see me.
BERT:	Well, that oughta make an outdoor man out of me. So long, Joanie. I gotta go now.

And so he went out of my life, Bert Lahr—the only man I ever loved.

But greater disappointments were in store for me. One night Rudy asked me if I'd like a seafood dinner. I said, "Yes." So, he came over to the house with a bag of salt water taffy. I felt sure he was going to propose, so I made up very carefully. What a time I had with that pancake make-up! The batter kept dripping in my eyes.

Then Rudy gave me the bad news. His duties in the Coast Guard obliged him to give up the Sealtest Village Store, so he was turning it over to me to run for him.

And so he went out of my life, Rudy Vallee—the only man I ever loved.

Well, with drooping spirits, I opened the Sealtest Store the next morning. It was so lonesome without Rudy, until the doorbell tinkled and who should enter but my childhood sweetheart, Jack Haley—the only man I ever loved.

"Joanie," he cried, "why, you've changed! You've grown up. You're a *woman*!"

"That's what I keep telling them down at the draft board," I replied.

Jack was so gallant. He said to me, "My, what a dapper outfit you're wearing." That was silly, of course, I haven't worn one of those things since I was a baby.

I started right in to convince Jack that he should stay and help me run the store. Yes, folks, that was the start of a beautiful friendship. Jack is the rugged, outdoor type of man, so I joined in all of his sports. One day we went salmon fishing. Jack asked me if I had ever hooked a salmon. I told him—no, but I once swiped a herring.

We went to the racetrack together, too. Jack had a swell system for betting, but one day it failed. He bet on a horse named Alcohol, and Alcohol ruined his system.

We went to the bull fights, too. I never knew what a picador was before, but I learned there. Every time I walked into a roomful of them, they'd each pick a door and beat it.

Oh, here comes a customer.

CUSTOMER:	Miss Davis, did you see Action in the North Atlantic?
JOAN:	I did.
CUSTOMER:	I thought you looked like you'd been torpedoed. Goodbye.

That's the nicest part of running a store. You meet only the best people. Oh, well, where was I?

Then came my great vindication in Court. Yes, I decided to sue Blossom Blimp for calling me homely, bowlegged, unattractive and a moron. I engaged Basil Rathbone—the famous Sherlock Holmes of the movies. Jack Haley came along to represent me, too. Gee, two men fighting for me. I felt like a quarter-pound of hamburger. There we were in the courtroom and Basil was speaking.

BASIL:	By the way, Miss Davis, I found two fellows to testify that you aren't homely.
JOAN:	You did?
BASIL:	Yes, but just as I talked them into coming to court to testify, they got into a terrible fight.
JOAN:	About what?

BASIL:	They couldn't decide which one was really Napoleon.
JOAN:	Two guys claiming they were Napoleon! Gee, one of them must have been crazy.
CRIER:	Order in the court. This court is now in session. Judge Rodney P. McGivney presiding.
JUDGE:	Come, come, leave us commence with the proceedings. Somebody hand me my gravel.
BASIL:	You mean your gavel.
JUDGE:	No, my gravel. I keep sliding off the bench. What's the first case?
JOAN:	Your Honor, I charge Blossom Blimp with libel. I charge her with slander. I charge her with malicious gossip. I charge her with . . .
JUDGE:	Just a minute. You got here a charge account?
HALEY:	I object. I stand on my constitutional rights.
JUDGE:	You can't stand on your constitutional rights.
HALEY:	Very well, then I'll sit on my ipso facto.
BASIL:	Your Honor, I'd like to question Mrs. Blimp. Now, Mrs. Blimp, have you any proof that Miss Davis is homely, bowlegged and stupid? . . . and I realize I'm a sucker for asking that question.
JUDGE:	Stop! I'm dismissing this case. Miss Davis, I judge all evidence by its face value, and, since your face has absolutely no value, the court is recessed—and besides my wife is having meat for dinner tonight.
BASIL:	Miss Davis, I'm afraid I can't help you any further.
JOAN:	But, Basil, how can you say that to the woman you love . . . the woman you're going to marry?
BASIL:	Just a moment. How did that word "marriage" slip into the conversation?

JOAN:	I didn't slip. I pushed it.
BASIL:	That settles it. I'm leaving. Good day.
JOAN:	Ah, there he goes, Basil Rathbone—the only man I ever loved!

Ho-hum, back to work in the Sealtest Village Store again. Wonder where the stepladder is. Jack Haley said to mark our prices as close to the ceiling as possible. Oh, here comes Jack now.

HALEY:	Say, Joan, you took forty-percent out of my pay last week. The withholding tax is only twenty.
JOAN:	No, Jack. Twenty percent is for a regular forty-hour week, but last week I worked you eighty hours, so it's twice as much.
HALEY:	Oh, I see. For a minute I thought I was being gypped. Say, what's all the manuscript? What have you been writing, Joan?
JOAN:	Oh, I've been writing the story of my life and loves, Jack.
HALEY:	I bet that contains a lot of typographical errors.
JOAN:	Gee, Jack. Here we are at the finish and we forgot to put in a commercial. Oh, boy, will Sealtest be sore!
HALEY:	Don't worry, Joan. We still have room, and, look, here comes John Laing now!

(Door Opens—Bell Tinkles)

LAING:	Say, Joan, I've got a complaint.
JOAN:	Hello, John. What's wrong?
LAING:	Well, every week I come to the Sealtest Village Store and all I ever do is tell people about Sealtest Milk and Ice Cream. I never get to tell any jokes. I never get any laughs.
JOAN:	Well, do you know any jokes, John?

LAING: Sure, I know a swell joke about two psychiatrists. It seems that two psychiatrists met on the street one day and one says to the other, "You're all right, today . . . how am I?"

JOAN: Yeah? And what did the other psychiatrist say?

LAING: No, no, Joan. The joke's over.

JOAN: Oh, the joke's over! Say, that's all right. What are you doing this time next week?

LAING: Why, nothing, Joan.

JOAN: You ain't kidding, brother.

LAING: Well, I guess I'd better stick to selling Sealtest Milk and Ice Cream. At least they always get laughs.

JOAN: Now, wait a minute. How do Sealtest Milk and Ice Cream get laughs?

LAING: Well, they help to build up health and energy. And when people are well, they are happy. And, when they're happy, they laugh.

JOAN: You can get quicker results with a feather.

LAING: Joan! Why, do you know that MILK, ICE CREAM and OTHER DAIRY PRODUCTS form one of the Seven Basic Food Groups which our Government urges us to have every day to maintain health on the Home Front? Yes, Sealtest Milk and Ice Cream are *two great foods*. They are rich in vitamins, minerals and proteins; rich in that quick energy value which keeps us fit for wartime tasks; rich in those food elements so essential to health. And—they have a tradition of quality and purity which millions of housewives sum up in this way: "When it's Sealtest, I *know* it's the finest."

Chapter 7
Hold That Ghost

Joan scored her biggest and most remembered film success as Camille Brewster, the female radio screamer, in Abbott and Costello's *Hold That Ghost* (1941). Originally titled *Oh, Charlie*, it was intended to be A&C's third picture, but after their huge smash hit *Buck Privates* (introducing the beat-defining "Boogie Woogie Bugle Boy"), Universal was eager to follow that up with another zippy Armed Forces musical, *In the Navy*. In fact, though there are a few songs in *Ghost*, these were added after the main film was shot to capitalize on the Andrews Sisters'/musical formula that worked so well for the comics before. Ted Lewis and his Orchestra were also added to the opening and ending scenes, though little was seen of him, and Joan Davis was not used in these. Director Arthur Lubin was hired for $5,000 on the day after *Buck Privates* was previewed, with the total cost of *Ghost* coming in at $190,000.

The action follows one-time waiters Chuck Murray (Bud Abbott) and Ferdie Jones (Lou Costello), who inherit a gangster's dilapidated speakeasy, since they are mistakenly with him at the time of his death. There was no money in the estate, since Moose Matson (William Davidson) always claimed he kept his fortune "in his head." The crime buddies he stiffed are certain the loot is hidden in the old house, and resort to scare tactics to frighten the boys, and their stranded, frightened guests (including Joan), out of the place as they search for the dough. Ultimately, Ferdie finds the great wad of cash in the moose's head hanging on the wall and foils the tough guys. The boys now have the money to open up that nightclub (with spa attached!) they've always wanted, with Ted Lewis and the Andrews Sisters singing for everyone else's supper.

The film's standout scene was certainly Joan's "Blue Danube" dance with Costello after dinner, in which she repeatedly strikes him on the head, splashes water on him, tosses him at an old piano, which he completely demolishes, and finally rumbas off with a wet washtub stuck on her tush. Dorothy Masters unwisely wrote in her *New York Daily News* review, "Joan Davis is on hand to bolster any weak spots in the film." Audiences didn't spot any weaknesses, naming it one of the biggest successes of the year, and, because of this, helped secure Abbott and Costello as the top moneymakers of 1941. *Film Daily*'s assessment was perfect, calling it "sure-fire riotous comedy that is a cinch to please and

Dancing with Lou Costello for the photographer of *Hold That Ghost,* **1941.**

should ring the box-office bell. *Hold That Ghost* is a cinch to please all those theater patrons who have become rabid A&C fans in the past few months. Lou Costello has never been funnier. At times his comedy is so fast that lines of dialogue are ignored and the audience roars at the pantomime he uses with his lines."

The biggest shock of the picture was the fact that such a financially successful collaboration did not result in a re-pairing of the team with Joan. It had worked for the Andrews Sisters, but for some ghostly reason, Joan wasn't even considered for any of their later top scare pictures, such as the fitting *Abbott and Costello Meet Frankenstein*. Of course, rarely would a female comic be given equal time for gags as Lou; it had happened in *Here Come the Co-eds* and *Keep 'Em Flying*, but it's possible that one clown per picture was all the studio could stand.

Yokel Boy (1942) wasn't a wise decision by the studios as a Joan Davis vehicle. Judy Canova had been the cornball hit of Lew Brown's musical Broadway show, but when Republic Pictures had difficulties with their star, Joan was brought in to pinch hit, and struck out with reviewers. The theme that seemed to hit everyone was that the picture tried too hard, and even the usual Davis-champion *Variety* had to state, "Miss Davis sadly overplays for the comedy." Another reviewer stated, "*Yokel Boy* works so hard to be funny, you can see the perspiration standing right out on its brow. And that ain't funny." The influential *Film Daily* praised, however, that "the production plays strictly for laughs. Nothing else matters very much. The story doesn't stand analysis, being as far-fetched as any yarn could possibly be. But the plot generates so much comedy–crazy, what-the-hell-is-the-difference comedy—much of which is on the slapstick side—that the story becomes of little consequence. Republic has chucked everything into this one to create laughs, with the result that sometimes *Yokel Boy* runs a little too wild in every direction."

Off the cuff of real-life gangster news, *Yokel Boy*'s plot hook was engagingly quirky. Ailing studio Mammoth Studios needs a few winning films under their belt and more positive press if they plan to remain open. Reading an odd news story about an Emoryville, Kansas man who knows how to guess which film will fill up his local cinema, executive producer R.B. Harris (Alan Mowbray) brings in Joe Ruddy (Eddie Foy, Jr.) to work his magic. One of his first brainstorms is to replace the actor who just quit their current *King of Crime* film with real gangster, Bugsie Malone (Albert Dekker), to play himself in a rewrite of the script. Through Malone's sister, Molly (Joan Davis), Joe tracks the tough guy down and, because he promised his sister to start going straight after his latest tussle with the law, he agrees to do the picture, with a *lot* of changes to make him, not the cops, the sympathetic character.

The studio goes through so much delay and budget hell with Malone that the studio pulls out and Bugsie agrees to put a million bucks he has hidden into it to finish the picture. Unfortunately, Molly is the only one who knows where the cash is hidden, and after a bump on the head to recall where it's located, she reverts to daffy childhood and has to be conked on the head again to snap out of it. Money found, and all ending as well as can be, the Malones hop a train back to Chicago, but not before they lure Joe onto the end of the train for a quick marriage ceremony. Molly is sure fast on the draw getting into that wedding dress . . .

There wasn't much Joan Davis in this one, but it was certainly one of her best supporting actress vehicles, especially her opening "Jim" song, written just for this film. One report states that nothing—not even the plot and characters—was left from the original Judy Canova-Buddy Ebsen musical once the studio bought it, except two songs, "It's Me Again" and "Comes Love." An unpublished story by Russell Rouse and real-life movie fan, Private Kenneth Wilkinson, who had seen 312 films in a year's time, were the basis. Stage beauty Betty Kean was Republic's first pick for the Molly role, but it went to Joan after Betty sprained her ankle, which delayed shooting from January 8 through the 14th. The film was shot between December 1941 and late January 1942, released on March 13, 1942.

Joan does her bit for the war effort.

On December 7, 1941 lives changed forever. The country was at war. Time on her hands and a new crisis on the homefront gave Joan ample opportunity for helping out with the new national emergency. Around April 22, 1942, ten soldiers from her hometown of St. Paul arrived, and, learning this, she and Si quickly invited them in for a weekend of fun. A few telephone calls rounded up some film colony friends (Eddie & June Norris, the Bob Livingstons, Joan Woodbury, Tim & Irene Ryan, the Grant Lamonts, Bert Lahr, Al Orsatti, the Paul Isaacsons, and the Mort Greens), and the entire party moved from the Wills' Coldwater Canyon home to Joan's ranch near Lake Enchanto. There they enjoyed swimming, baseball, horseback riding, and finally a barbecue dinner.

Joan did what she could for the war effort, including having a weekly draw for her soldier guests in her radio audience to win a free telephone call to his family or sweetheart.

Chapter 8
Joanie's Tea Room

Sometime in the early '40s the Wills-Davis household changed addresses, opting for a slightly smaller Bel-Air home (in the beautiful hills above the University of California) that was closer to the studio. It had reportedly been used for exterior scenes in *The Philadelphia Story* (1940). They bought two adjoining acres and had a "good-sized" swimming pool built, which gave Joan plenty of exercise running the 200 feet uphill from the pool to answer telephone calls. It took them a while to arrange an extension cord that long.

Always a clever business woman, she paid for that pool by always thinking ahead. In June of 1942 she was seeking a copyright for the use (via television) of the game "Indications," which was sweeping Hollywood almost like the gin rummy craze.

At the end of June, she gave her mother a surprise "welcome home" party after Nina spent the last two months visiting hometown St. Paul. When "Mother" arrived home that night, none of the lights in her daughter's home would light. Just as she gave up, flashlights suddenly pierced the darkness and cries of welcome came from the assembled guests, which included Dewey Robinson and wife, Nancy Kelly, Eddie Norris and Patti Clare, Addison Richard and his wife, Mr. and Mrs. Tim Ryan, and others. From there, the "blackout" party proceeded to the patio, where a barbecue dinner was served with the moon and flashlights giving the only light. Later, Joan started an amusing new game called "Blackout Quiz." She liked her games.

The next month, Joan—and Si—also took a return trip to St. Paul. She had accepted an invitation from her former school teacher, Mrs. Jeanette Slocum, to debate with local students on whether an inexperienced boy or girl should risk coming to Hollywood to get an acting job in films.

Joan took the negative side of the argument. (It was easy for her at the moment; she was in negotiations with Columbia to sell her life story for a film plot. But the studio didn't bite hard enough.) She also discovered 18-year-old protégé Dorothy Porer at the Dryden Little Theater and promised to bring her out to Hollywood; somehow, that ultimately defeated her argument, though.

Sweetheart of the Fleet, filmed from February 20 through March 9, 1942 and released on May 21, is one of Joan's most energetic wartime romps, this time for Columbia Pictures. She's Phoebe Weyms, secretary to dreamboat Gordon Crouse (Tim Ryan), an ad executive who needs some prodding to discover the stars in her eyes for him. So, as a way of impressing him, she decides to unmask the "Blind Date Girls," Brenda (Blanche Stewart) and Cobina (Elvia Allman), hit singers on the hugely popular radio series, *A Blind Date with Romance.* Navy officers Lt. Philip Blaine (William Wright) and Ensign George "Tip" Landers (Robert Stevens) are hot for her idea that this should happen in front of a recruiting rally, but Crouse thinks it's a lousy notion, especially since the girls have clock-stopping faces. Undaunted, Phoebe merely hires hot models Jerry Gilbert (Jinx Falkenburg) and Kitty Leslie (Joan Woodbury) to pose as the purring duet while the real singers provide sound for their lip synchs. Of course, the real BD Girls want something for their trouble: sailor boyfriends. When the guys find out the truth and elope with the singers, Phoebe's in a pickle on the night of the big rally, but phones them in Connecticut, where they're honeymooning, and has them sing their songs from a radio station there. After the show's a hit, the truth is explained and the impressed Crouse takes his secretary in his arms.

Tim Ryan, Joan Davis and the "famous radio comics" Brenda and Cobina in *Sweetheart of the Fleet*, Columbia, 1942.

Film Daily wrote that "*Sweetheart of the Fleet* contains entertainment out of all proportion to the modesty of the production. With Joan Davis and Brenda and Cobina mixed up in it, it is bound to have plenty of laughs and a fair share of insanity. Some of the comedy is surprisingly good, and the story has a number of clever twists. The masculine customers will find the presence in the cast of Jinx Falkenburg and Joan Woodbury an additional lure. Both gals are extremely easy on the optics."

Not only was it reported that Joan was writing her own comedy songs for *Sweetheart*, but that she was casting little 8-year-old Beverly in the sequel to that picture, playing her kid sister. Bev was being groomed; at an Easter egg hunt at Mrs. & Mrs. Robert Young's place, Joan talked to Irving Asher about giving her daughter a screen test at MGM. She could be as political as anyone when it came to a career for herself, and Bev.

And she was busy supplementing her film time making just as many public appearances. She and hubby Si appeared with just about everyone else in Hollywood at the California State Guard Military Ball at the Palladium on April 15, 1942. She used those appearances to try out new comedy material that she and Si were coming up with. At the Biltmore Bowl in mid-April, Joan was quoted as saying, "The man who brags that he runs things at his house, usually means the lawnmower, the washing machine, the vacuum cleaner, the baby carriage and the errands."

In August of 1942 Joan, Rudy Vallee, Jane Withers, Kay Kyser, Dick Mack and the late John Barrymore were part of a 11-minute short for Columbia, *Screen Snapshots*, that featured a section of Joan's radio show, as broadcast in front of the San Diego Marine Base and Long Beach Naval Reserve Aviation Base. It was Barrymore's last screen appearance in front of Hollywood cameras.

Strong critical acclaim, and an audience always hungry for more, left Joan in a dexterous position to up the ante on her new film contract. For $75,000 a picture, she signed with RKO and Universal for two years (1944-46), putting her approximately $10,000 over what other supporting stars were pulling in major studios.

If picture work was sporadic, at least radio kept Joan in the public ear. She lined up guest stars galore when her radio series returned for another season on August 31, 1944: Eddie Cantor, Rudy Vallee, Johnny Mercer, Arthur Lake, Kenny Baker, plus the usuals: The Fountaineers and Eddie Paul and his Orchestra. *Variety* was strangely unimpressed, citing that "timing seems to have gone wrong with this one giving evidence that not enough preparation was given to the first fall show. Idea of Miss Davis' Christmas tree and party for overseas G.I.s, while laudable enough, just couldn't carry the running story."

Together with Vallee, Roy Rogers, Victor Borge and others, Joan appeared on *Hi-Jinks of 1942*, a "public show" at the Wilshire-Ebell Theater, benefitting the Valley Jewish Community Center, on June 5, 1942. The musical night was produced by radio producer/songwriter Dick Mack.

He's My Guy (1943) was another musical loan-out to Universal, from the same *Hold That Ghost/Buck Privates* mold that was so hot in wartime. With plenty of swing, including Burton Lane's "The Boogie-Woogie-Boogie Man" and the title song by Don Raye and Gene DePaul, the film took a mere two weeks to film during November and December 1942, released the following March 26. It was an exhilarating 65-minute feature that made Joan a part of the plot for a change.

Working in a defense plant, Madge Donovan (Joan Davis) is friends with newlywed vaudeville team, Van Moore (Dick Foran) and Terry Allen (Irene Hervey). When their booker tells them that they aren't as good as their more famous vaudeville parents, Terry wants to quit showbiz and joins Madge working at the plant. Her boss loves Terry's idea of putting on a show to boost the workers' moral, but Madge has to pretend that Van is *her* husband so that Van can produce and direct the show. It almost breaks up the real marriage. And when that heel boss Kirk (Don Douglas) tries to take credit with his boss that the show was all his idea, Madge tells the truth and Terry joins Van on stage for a wow show that's so spiffy it ultimately makes the couple co-directors of entertainment for all the Marsden plants in the country.

Motion Picture Herald thought that Joan "lifts this minor musical by its budgetary bootstraps and she stirred its Hollywood preview audience to more laughter than many a production costing a dozen times as much money." *Film Daily* wrote that this "is another of Universal's fast-stepping, inconsequential swing musicals geared to the tastes of the young folks. The film packs loads of fun and entertainment for audiences for which this type of diversion is created . . . The cast performs with vim and vigor, especially Joan Davis."

Though named as an obvious sequel to *Two Latins from Manhattan, Two Senoritas from Chicago* (1943) put Joan back into a similar situation with a different job and character name. She is Daisy Baker, garbage sorter at a Portuguese hotel with ambitions of being a theatrical agent. When she finds a tossed out musical play in the trash, she sends it to New York where it's promptly snatched up by producer Robert Shannon (Emory Parnell). But creating a

Douglas Leavitt, Frank O'Connor, Joan and Emory Parnell in
***Two Senoritas from Chicago*, 1943.**

fictional author, Manuel DeBraganza, starts trouble when he's needed to sign the contract. So Daisy invents two sisters for him, Gloria (Jinx Falkenburg) and Maria (Ann Savage), hotel maids who really want to be musical comedy stars, who have legal power to sign the contract. All goes awry when they push to play the leads and the original authors sell their musical to a rival producer. Jailed for hoodwinking, all works out eventually when it's decided to put on a *new* musical; of course, Daisy, who escaped jail to come view opening night, is finally caught by the cops as the curtain comes down.

The New York Post wrote, "Joan Davis, a comic figure and not pretty, furnishes the laughs and some relief from all the beauty."

Those ugly cracks hurt. More than once Joan considered having a nose job and going the regular starlet route; in 1944 it was reported she did, to correct her nose being "a little bit out of symmetry," as she put it. Her figure was fine, according to all, but on August 19, 1949 she told reporters she was finally going to do the plastic surgery. "I've been on the verge of this for a long time. I think all women would prefer beauty to brains or courage or wealth or any other quality or possession heaven might grant. I would myself. And like all clowns I have a yen to play Macbeth or something equally dramatic. In years past I've gone right up to the hospital steps and then backed down. This time I'm going through with the deal—new face, new personality and all." She never did.

According to a *Photoplay* article, lack of classical good looks didn't stop Joan from being just as popular with all the handsome guys around the set. When asked about her appeal, one honest man answered, "Because, since Joan has no beauty to fuss over, primp over, worry over, her mind is free from herself at all times. What we are saying is more important to Joan than how she arches her brows or twinkles her eyelashes when she replies. Because she sheds movies like a duck sheds water, and because she's interested in every topic that interests a man."

The swingin' RKO revue picture, *Around the World*, filmed from May to July 1943 and released the following April, followed the world tour of Kay Kyser and his orchestra, comic Mischa Auer and man-hungry Joan Davis (all playing "themselves") around the world entertaining our wartime troops, with lots of bright songs by Jimmy McHugh and Harold Adamson. After falling into the orchestra pit without saying a word in the opening scene, Joan's part of the plot comes in Egypt when Mischa urges her to wear an engagement ring so she can seem hard to get. It works. But the three men she attracts, who turn out to be enemy agents, are mostly attracted to the ring which has a secret compartment containing a map.

Originally entitled *Keep 'Em Singing*, the prologue after the opening credits read: "To every battle front where men and women of the United Nations fight—civilians from all walks of life are contributing their honest efforts to the struggle. Among these, the brightest stars of Hollywood and Broadway do their bit—we welcome you to come along on this tour of the global conflict. So stand by!"

One of many hat gag photos made for *Around the World*, 1943.

The *Los Angeles Examiner* gave the tour its due by calling it "a funny, peppy and active vaudeville show with Army camp backgrounds. Kay Kyser has an ingratiating screen personality and does almost as well by himself in the movies as he does on the radio. Joan Davis is an inimitable clown and is very amusing as the gal continually looking for romance." *The Christian Science Monitor* wrote, "Miss Davis keeps the laughter going in her athletic fashion, diving over the footlights at one point and being bounced out of a jeep at another. She can clown with the best of them in a comic song." And *The New York Times* posed the murky question, "How does one say that the humor dished up by Joan Davis and Misha Auer is straight off the cob, without offending those fellows who will probably think it swell?"

The *Los Angeles Examiner* ran the following short article at the time: "Joan Davis, the original 'fall girl' of the movies, still takes her own tumbles, and despite the countless falls and flops she has performed before the cameras has never been seriously hurt. In *Around the World*, starring Kay Kyser and his band, the premier comedienne escaped one of the most difficult stunts of her career—a comedy fall into the orchestra pit from a five-foot high stage. Joan executed this intricate fall to the complete satisfaction of director Allan Dwan in a single take, and without a rehearsal. Four movie cameras recorded the action from various angles to insure getting it in one take. Incidentally, Joan claims that had she been paid for her union scale commanded by stunt-girls, she would be a millionairess today."

Apparently loosely based on Eddie Cantor's debut at Miner's Burlesque Theatre in 1908, *Show Business* was also Cantor's first producing credit for RKO; he was originally to write its screenplay as a vehicle starring Cary Grant and Dinah Shore. The blithesomely nostalgic musical instead teamed Cantor and Joan as supporting comics to love-leads George Murphy and Constance Moore.

"In the colorful era of belles, bloomers and beers in buckets," begins the film's prologue, "trouped ambitious groups of loveable hams known as show folks, all dreaming of the Big Time. In the burlesque theatres of those days were born many of today's great stars. Such a theatre was Miner's Bowery . . ."

It is 1914 when burlesque headliner and notorious ladies' man George Doane (Murphy) decides to give bulging-eyed singer Eddie Martin (Cantor) tips on how to improve his frightened amateur debut. Encouraged and elated on winning first prize, Eddie accompanies George to Kelly's Café where they meet "sister" act Constance Ford (Moore) and Joan Mason (Davis). George falls for Connie instantly, and after dancing together, the four decide to team up and save enough money to open in big-time vaudeville with a whole new act. George is in love and keeps harping on Connie to marry him, as does Joan to Eddie. Eventually George and Connie tie the knot, but on the night Connie is going to have a baby, George is waylaid by an old girlfriend (Nancy Kelly), and all is over by the time he makes it to the hospital to find out that she lost the baby.

Devastated by the lost of a wife and child, George loses himself in wartime entertaining and is on the skids after the war, singing for drinks when Eddie finally tracks him down. Connie never remarried and after hearing him sing their song, "It Had to Be You," on stage one night, it's as if time never passed. In a double wedding, George remarries Connie and Joan finally gets her Eddie, and the last line: "I *love* that boy!"

There are songs a-plenty along the way, including Cantor-hits "Makin' Whoppee" (with enough eye rolling to sizzle censors) and a prancing, hand-clapping "Dinah." But the standout performance of the entire film is without a doubt the absurd opera (sextette from *Lucia di Lammermoor*) spoof, in which the gang eats bananas while lip synching to a record on an old Victrola which ultimate winds down, then skips, giving big-bosommed Joan ample schtick before dragging everyone (including the St. Bernard dog who is there for no reason) off on the tail of her dress.

Released in May of 1944, the RKO film was shot from late October to December 1943. *The New York Herald Tribune* oddly commented that "Miss Davis is sometimes a bit too colorful, though, as a foil for Cantor, she is less

Joan, Beverly, Jack Haley and his son at the premiere of *Show Business*.

raucous than usual." *Variety* thought that "there are plenty of laugh lines and situations, with the horseplay ideally set up between Cantor and Miss Davis. It's all for laughs, and several oldies are brushed up a bit to still catch attention from the customers due to spontaneous delivery and smart timing." Much praise was usually given over to the wealth of elder, popular songs given a proper airing. Though *Motion Picture Herald* had high hopes for it, calling it "the type of entertainment the public is craving, and it is good, too," it soon called it "one of the biggest disappointments we have had. Was sure we would do over our average preferred time gross, but fell several percent below. Guess Cantor can't drag 'em in anymore here. The picture was swell and one of the best musicals from RKO in some time."

The gala premiere at Grauman's Chinese Theater was attended by everyone from Ava & Eva Gardner to Lucille Ball, with the full rake in of $8,000 going to the soldiers' fund at Birmingham General Hospital. Fifty convalescing soldiers appeared at the premiere, each accompanied on the arm by an actress. Rudy

Vallee's Coast Guard band played before the screening and for "a musical interlude." Outside, many luminaries of the film and social world took bows at the microphone and wished Eddie well before eager, cheering fans. The event also celebrated Cantor's 35th year in show business; and his first stint as film producer.

The *Los Angeles Examiner* acknowledged that "as a producer, Eddie Cantor holds star Eddie Cantor down more than any other producer has ever attempted or achieved. The result is Cantor's best screen appearance [not the first review to express this opinion]. I never thought I'd live to write the description of 'under playing' to Cantor—but I swear he almost achieves it when he isn't in his typical song and dance mood. Joan Davis is supposed to be the 'plain' gal who loves Eddie and their hit and miss romance carries most of the laughs. But I thought Joan looked pretty—and she's just about tops among the nonchalant comediennes. Her aside to the audience about how much she loves Eddie is funny stuff."

At the time, Joan told *Silver Screen* magazine of her hectic Fox schedule: "It was a matter of dashing from set to set, changing costumes and makeup on the way. I made 22 films at Fox in five years! And I'm still waiting for the perfect dramatic picture. I've never yet been the victim of a great script, in fact, most of my stuff has had more to do with caricature than character."

Shot from October 15 to November 13, 1943, *Beautiful But Broke* wasn't released until January 28, 1944 but proved to be one of Joan's most versatile and musical offerings of the war years. As secretary to a theatrical agent who enlists in the Army, Dottie Duncan (Joan) is left to cope with the sticky business of providing male bands in a world that has them all enlisted in the military. The farce ensues when Dottie has two of her girls, Sally Richards (Jane Frazee) and Sue Ford (Judy Clark), sing over the phone for a club owner in Cleveland, pretending to be part of the all-girl band playing, but which is really a record. Once she's sold the band, she has to find one. So, Dottie hires Birdie Benson (Grace Hayle) and her all-girl band and the troupe head out to Cleveland by train. But when the girls decide to surrender their seats to twelve pilots in need of transportation, they are stuck in San Madero, Nevada. Dottie loses her purse (containing their train tickets) and the girls are evicted from the hotel due to lack of finances. Homeless, they plunk down into an abandoned house that is a munitions target and are shelled into thinking they're being invaded. Supervisor Bill Drake (John Hubbard) feels terrible about the situation and invites the girls to stay at his apartment. Since the women of San Madero have defense plant jobs and have to leave their children unattended during the day, Bill suggests the girls give a benefit concert to raise money to build a daycare center. It's a smash and attracts national press, leading the Cleveland manager to give them trouble about never showing up at his club. Bill admits that he had their train tickets the whole time, but pleads with Dottie not to go. A few of the girls have fallen for local lugs and soon all the girls decide to stay in Nevada.

The film, originally entitled *Beautiful But Nice*, packed a lot of song into a mere 72 minutes, belting out Big Band renditions of favorites such as "Pistol

A scene from *Beautiful But Broke*, 1944.

Packin' Mama" and "Shoo Shoo Baby" as well as typical WWII titles of "Mr. Jive Has Gone to War" and "Keeping it Private."

Motion Picture Herald was ecstatic, calling it "a whale of a job . . . It's funny all the way and my patrons laughed so hard that you could not hear the sound at times. Give us more of these, Columbia; it's just what the doctor ordered. Joan is the funniest thing on the air and screen; she is just a natural comedienne who knows her onions."

Kansas City Kitty was a delightful Columbia vehicle that ran a good 63 minutes on high octane. Her third film of 1944 was also one of her funniest and was the first feature for director Del Lord.

Shifty music publishers, Joe Lathim (Robert Emmett Keane) and Dave Clark (Tim Ryan), strong-arm piano teacher Polly Jasper (Joan Davis) into their ailing business as a song plugger. When cowboy Jeff Williker (John Bond) steps into the office to play his catchy "Kansas City Kitty" for the gang, the trio jumps at it, giving him (via tricking the landlord for the money) $200 for full rights to the song. It's an immediate hit. Polly takes tens of thousands of orders for the song, but when the publishers realize they're being sued by the author of "Minnesota Minnie," which claims to have the same melody, they scat after bilking Polly for a few thousand bucks to buy the business.

Touching her friend, singer Eileen Hasbrook (Jane Frazee), for the balance of the required cash, the girls set up business, only to quickly learn of the lawsuit. Polly thinks she can deter the suing songwriter, Oscar Lee (Matt Willis), by coming on with sex appeal and plenty of chicken pie. She wants to strangle the guy, though, the more she has to put up with his ultra-corny jokes and is forced

Kansas City Kitty, 1944.

to ignore her real dreamboat, dentist Henry Talbot (Erik Rolf). When she can't juggle both guys over separate dinner tables, Lee storms out and the case goes to court, where Dr. Talbot proves that both tunes were based upon a hundred-year-old song. [The same premise as Warners' *Naughty But Nice* (1939).] The case is dismissed and the would-be songwriting judge plays his own composition for Polly. It's "California Carrie," and yes, it's got the same melody as her Kitty. For that, Polly just has to give two good whacks on his bald noggin with the gavel.

The New York Post was less pleased than audiences: "But what can they [the cast] do when Joan Davis is the star and sees a chance to make faces? She makes some of the worst faces you've ever seen. Oddly enough, at other angles, she reminds you a little of Irene Dunne." Yet, Joan is "not worth the acute boredom of seeing the rest of the film." *Hollywood Citizen News* donated the flipside: "Joan Davis holds the spotlight from beginning to end and is ably supported by a pleasing cast, good music, and bright dialogue. Fortified with a semblance of endless versatility and a natural flair for comic delivery, Joan's box office value should rise sky high with more of these films. There's plenty of laughs in Monte Brice's dialogue and Del Lord's direction adds punch to the many situations."

Motion Picture Herald printed two completely different views in their "What the Picture Did for Me" column; on May 26, 1945, A.L. Dove struck with: "If I wrote my comments on this picture they would not print them. It fits in the lower bracket of a very poor double bill. It has no entertainment value. It was really a grand flop. I got stung very badly with this one." And to prove not all critics agree, James L. Johnson, a week later, wrote, "Joan gets funnier every time. She kept the audience laughing through the complete picture. We want more of these."

Radio work was thriving. *Movieland* picked Joan as the number one comedienne of 1944, after a Crossley (radio) rating of 32.4—the highest rating ever achieved by a woman. She was also making guest spots on some of the biggest shows in radio: *People Are Funny, National Barn Dance, Hedda Hopper's Hollywood, Blondie, Al Pearce Fun Valley, Duffy's Tavern, The Eddie Cantor Show,* Bing Crosby's program, and more.

Art Linkletter (top), Ed Gardner (Archie on *Duffy's Tavern*) and Joan on *People Are Funny*.

She had a great gag for appearing on these shows: on her own Sealtest show one week, guest star Edward Everett Horton told Joan that there was a package for her that she'd have to find. She looked for that darn package on show after show; it was finally handed to her on December 16, 1943 by Eddie Cantor on his show. It contained her Queen of Comedy crown, a deserving present considering that her listening audience had grown to an amazing 115 million listeners for that week of show-hopping.

Andy Russell proclaims Joan "Queen of Radio."

To explain her success, she took over for the vacationing Erskine Johnson and supplied a "What Makes a Comedian" essay for the *Los Angeles Illustrated News* on October 7, 1944.

Ever see the inside of a comic's brain?

You haven't? Okeh. Tell you what I'm going to do. I'm going to show you my brain. Don't laugh, I'm serious—or does that strike you funny?—comics do have brains. Take mine for instance. It's a nice brain. Frequently it works like a clock—first it goes tick, then tock! Funniest sound you've ever heard.

Pull up a microscope and let's look. As the microscope is slowly adjusted, out of the distant horizon we see that my brain has two parts. One side says a joke is funny. The other side says it's not funny. It got me so mixed up I hired an umpire to tell me the score. Do you know what the score was? It was 0—0!

Seriously, that is how a comedian's brain is made. Actually, one side doesn't say a joke is funny. That side is the brain file. The other side that argues is better judgement. Here's something you didn't know. Before a comedian tells a joke he has actually (within the space of a few split seconds) five to ten jokes out of his brain file. His better judgement argues until the right joke fits the situation, then better judgement laughs and releases that joke to the comic's mouth.

Advertising for Swan Soap.

Let's prove this. Take another look through the microscope. You'll see that the brain is built like a machine and notice my file side closely. Whenever I need a joke (and I sure need one now) a brain messenger presses a button and a joke pops down a shoot. Three wheels start going around and if they stop on two cherries and a lemon, five jokes drop out. Someday I'm going to hit the jackpot and clean up.

Speaking of cleaning up. A comedian continually cleans old jokes from his brain. Just like when you clean house, you usually find a lot of old rags, bottles, newspapers and junk. I gave my brain a housecleaning recently, and guess what I found: old rags, bottles, newspapers and junk!

Only one trouble about a comic's brain: Quite often your judgement goes on vacation. That's when a comic types himself by his jokes. Every story that comes out of his brain has the same formula. Recently, this happened to me. It was when the armed forces were awarding pretty girls special titles. The laugh part of my brain immediately gave me jokes like: "I've been voted Miss Tank Top of '44!" These jokes got me a lot of laughs. It kept on until suddenly I realized they had gone too far on this formula. I held a housecleaning and got rid of that type of joke.

Look again at my brain. Here's a pair of smoked glasses to ease the glare on your eyes. Adjust the microscope to the file part. You'll see jokes there to fit any situation. Whenever I want a joke about the weather, all I do is tip the brain messenger, go ahead, tip the brain messenger, he could use an extra quarter—and see what happens. Out comes a joke about the weather: "It's been so hot, when I went home the other day, I saw some ice cubes taking a shower!"

All comics' brains work that way. One comedian toured so many army camps and told so many service stories, every one of his jokes have chevrons. Another comic I know has so many jokes in his brain, he has no room to think, so his brain moved out. After all, the guy went over the ceiling—sorta blew his top!

Don't misunderstand and think that a comic's brain file only contains jokes she's heard from other comedians. That's not true. A lot of comics construct their own jokes and after getting a laugh, store them away to be used in the right situation. Comedians have several types of brains. There's the comic whose brain is very fertile. Instead of jokes, he grows radishes, turnips and greens. But most comics are not vegetarians, they live off of laughs.

That brings me up to the third part of a comedian's brain. Turn your microscope lightly to the west. You'll see a coin box that resembles a pay telephone. Our brain file puts a joke into the slot, if we get a laugh, bell rings and we get the right number or audience reaction. My machine only failed me once. I told a joke one night, a bell rang, and I got the wrong number. That's what I get for using a slug!

Jack Haley wasn't really needed as a straight man, so *Joanie's Tea Room* (and later, with the same tea theme, *Joan Davis Time*) began in the mid-40s for sponsor Lever Brothers ("makers of Swan Soap!"), serving up some of her strongest radio shows. The usual recipe in the *Tea Room* begins with low-wailing Harry Von Zell, announcer, moaning, "Poor Joan . . . ain't got nobody . . . She's nobody's sweetheart now . . .," followed by a maniacal, hugely unsympathetic laugh. After the introductions of crooner Andy Russell, energetic oldie Verna Felton, cagey, romantic competition Shirley Mitchell, "the music of Paul Weston and his orchestra, and yours Swanlyserely, Harry Von Zell," Joan is introduced as America's Queen of Comedy—followed by a huge roar of laughter from the audience. Harry then shouts to Joan cautious quips like "Come on, Joan, stop it,

Joanie and announcer Harry Von Zell.

give that violin player back his toupee! Stop playing football with it, he'll catch cold!" Once the story begins, a muted trumpet mimics what Joan says after the phone rings: "Joanie's tea room. Joan Davis speaking." Between taunting the ever-large Rosela Hipperton (Verna), who weighs a ton and has the hots for Harry, and scratching after Andy (matching claws often with Shirley), Joan has plenty of opportunities for squeaking out some clever gaffaws.

10-year-old Beverly rehearses with Joan for *Joanie's Tea Room*, CBS, 1945.

Having peaked her radio show as the #3 comedy program in the country, Joan was able to sign another $1 million contract with Lever Brothers when she switched over from NBC to CBS. When she began pitching for Swan Soap, it was reported that "Radio's Queen of Comedy" was third only to Bob Hope and Jack Benny as radio's highest paid star.

The King (Bob Hope) and Queen of Radio Comedy.

For that kind of money, Swan was pulling out all the stops to promote their new man-hungry soap latherer. Thus, sudsy ads such as:

"ATTRACTING A MAN IS A CINCH!"
SAYS JOAN DAVIS
LAFF-LOVELY CBS RADIO STAR HEARD MONDAY NIGHTS

1. One good way is to lasso any man, drag him within easy reach, and put your foot on the back of his Adam's apple.

   Of course after two or three days your foot may get tired. So you'll probably prefer the *mild* technique I've worked out with that wonderful, new, white floating Swan Soap. There's nothing like Swan to help you get along with men. For instance . . .

2. Take my grocer. (Is *he* a dream!) The other day I told him, "Shopping's tough but I can get along without lots of different soaps—long as I've got Swan! Swan's my One-and-Only for complexion, bath, dishes, laundry!"

"You're pretty smart!" he says. Hear that? Right away he's telling me *I'm pretty*!

3. Then last night my boyfriend phoned. "Joanie," he says, "I can't go through with our date!"

   "Mac!" I cried. "I've been Swanning my complexion just for you! Mild Swan helps babies' skin stay beautiful—so imagine what Swan's done for me! I'm a dream!" "*This* I have *got* to see," says Mac. Isn't it wonderful how Swan saved my romance?

4. Swan helps me give wonderful parties. While I relax in the living room, the boys just *flock* to the kitchen to Swan the dishes. If I get lonely, I go in and tell 'em how Swan swishes into dishpan suds faster than other floating soaps. I show 'em how soft 'n white Swan helps keep my hands. Then they show me snapshots of their girlfriends. We have a beautiful understanding!

5. I can't promise that Swan'll help you get along with men as well as I do. But you'll adore Swan 'cause it's *four swell soaps in one*! Simply stupendous for complexion, bath, dishes, and laundry! Switch to Swan . . . and switch your radio dial my way, too.

   I play Joan Davis on THE JOAN DAVIS SHOW (Imagine!), featuring Andy Russell, CBS, Monday Nights. Tune in!

Taking over George Burns & Gracie Allen's 8:30-9:00 p.m. spot on Mondays, the format remained pretty much the same when it began in September 1945. Crooner Andy Russell was a new feature, to cut the comedy a bit and give audiences time to reach for their Swan Soap. It was Joan who hired Russell ("I wanted to get the bobby-soxers; in fact, I wanted to get the whole damn family in"), but she was expected to hire singers, musicians and her own announcer from that $1 million paycheck; in fact, the total cost of the show was to be deducted from her salary, leaving her with an undisclosed profit. It was the real start of Joan the Business Woman, which would exercise her executive skills for running a hit TV series. A byproduct was that some co-workers and family members called her cheap or tight and difficult to deal with at times.

She awakened at 5:00 a.m., daily, no matter what. A secretary wheeled in a table with an extra cover that overlapped the bed, while Joan showered. After a lite breakfast, if working on a picture, she would drive to the studio and work until 6:00 p.m., then plunge into her nightly radio work: rehearsals, script-readings, and the unending executive decisions of dealing with the problems of musicians, writers and actors.

The burden of work wasn't completely hers, luckily. Though their personal relationship was severed, the Wills-Davis professional collaboration continued. Not only did Si brunt a large chuck of the daily work and household chores, but they had hired a couple, "sturdily independent folk from the hills of Tennessee," to act as butler and maid to the seven-room home.

Tearoom's workload paid off. *The New York World Telegram* rightly stated that "you probably won't even detect any difference [from the previous series]. We have Miss Davis . . . running a tearoom instead of a general store . . . Modes in comedy may come and go but Miss Davis remains the good-humored lass, uneasy about having so much virtue so long . . . Blessed with a sense of timing that is nothing short of sublime, Joan Davis remains one of the best comediennes in the business."

Another November 22, 1945 review gives a rundown of a typical show: "The show signs on. Paul Weston, the sedate-looking ork leader, jumps up and starts conducting with two long index fingers which he seems to be trying to pound into a jelly on an imaginary table top. Von Zell introduces Joan. The entire cast falls on their faces and salaam with hands. Verna Felton is down and can't get up, so Judge Hooker and Andy Russell pick her up, her bonnet askew on her conk. That business produces the laugh listeners hear when the show takes the air.

"From there on the show is all Joan. For one of Hollywood's fussiest and toughest actresses in rehearsals, she's a surprise on the air. So much at ease in front of the mike, and when the others are reading their lines, she rubber-legs off into the wings, coming out unusually often tonight to mug at the dumb audience and point at her script. Old Verna gets as many laughs as Joan because she hams up her stuff, and when she and Andy Russell have dialogue she keeps her arm around Andy's waist."

The show was consistently funny, with solid writing and an interesting contradiction in Joanie's character. Sure, she was chronically man-crazy, but roving

Hamming up "Mammy" for guest Al Jolson.

Swan Soap pitcher Harry Von Zell kept making a play for her. She wouldn't bite. "But after all, Joanie," he would shyly intone, "I'm a man, and you're a woman . . ." "Oh, Harry," she would reply, "you're always exaggerating." Her heart was aflutter for the young singer, regardless of southern belle Barbara Weatherby's (Shirley Mitchell) amorous, sometimes underhanded advances toward the single beau. Lucky for Joanie Harry is kept on his toes by staying out of the path of his heavy "girlfriend" Rosela Hipperton—Hippy to her friends—(Verna Felton), who always greets her own name with a teenage-energized "Hell-*lo*!" Joanie quips on Hippy constantly to keep the big girl down to earth, such as the time she boasts of taking long walks, asking Harry if she looks fit. Joanie admits, "Yeah, fit. F A T, fit."

Chapter 9
Slowing Down

R adio didn't take every waking hour.

She Gets Her Man (1945) was a 70-minute solid yuk Universal release, filmed from mid-October through mid-November of the previous year.

There's a blowgun murderer at large in Clayton! City leaders are being killed! Newspaper publisher Henry Wright (Donald MacBride) has the bright idea to send his reporting ace Breezy Barton (William Gargan) to Horsetroft, Nevada to bring back the only daughter of the previous chief of police, Ma Pilkington, after Brodie (Cy Kendall), sings the deceased Ma's praises to the public. The fact that daughter Pilky (Joan Davis) is as bright as a dark light and keeps accusing the wrong people of the crime doesn't matter; Brodie simply attaches the equally ineffectual Mulligan (Leon Errol), a cop, to her every step. After a few false

Joan and Leon Errol in *She Gets Her Man*, 1945.

accusations and a run in with gangsters, Pilky finally thwarts the mystery and nabs the culprit red-and-hypodermic handed. Of course, she's not sure if she should go back to Horsetroft just then. The good folk there have sent her a telegram offering to buy her an expensive house in Clayton if she'll just stay there.

The *New York Times* wasn't satisfied with having Joan in a more-than-comic-foil role. "Miss Davis is an able lady comic in brief supporting roles, especially, but she's rather hard to take in large, raw doses." *Motion Picture Herald* reported the heads of the coin: "Murders reach an amazing total in this mystery comedy, but never seem more than another gag routine for the antics of Joan Davis. The comedienne is allowed a bit of everything from smart dialogue to slapstick and manages them all in the frantic, good-humored style which has become her trademark. Old as the gags and situations are, a conscientious objector could hardly escape a couple of laughs . . . She carries the show, whipping herself into a brave stand, driving an idea to its unnatural conclusion and resisting sobriety in favor of speed and wisecracks."

Film Daily wrote that "the comic spirit of Joan Davis triumphs over the indifferent material at her disposal to make *She Gets Her Man* pretty good fun for the family trade. Intelligence has been booted into the background in the determination to squeeze as much laughter as possible out of the script. Under Erle C. Kenton's direction the action, which is not above descending to slapstick, is furious and constant."

George White's Scandals in 1945 had nothing to do with the previous 1934 film of the same name (as it, indeed, went by the working title of *George White's Scandals of 1945*), but it was very significant in the Davis household. The press devoted lots of column inches to the fact that Beverly Wills played Joan in a flashback scene, giving Bev one of her best feature scenes in her entire career.

Little Bev as little Joan in *George White's Scandals*, 1945.

Joan Mason (Joan Davis) and her betrothed Jack Evans (Jack Haley) attend a reunion of the Scandals Club, consisting of all those showgirls who appeared in George White's Scandals through the years. It's too bad wet blanket Clarabelle (Margaret Hamilton) is holding her brother Jack to the promise he made on his mother's death bed: Clarabelle has to be married before he can be. At least things are better for the true lovers of the story, show manager Tom McGrath (Phillip Terry) and Jill Ashbury (Martha Holliday), daughter of a previous Scandals dancer. Even though she chases Tom and is engaged to English nobleman Lord Asbury, she gets her man in the end; as does Joan, when an accidental sandbag on the head finally produces an optimistic Clarabelle.

Margaret Hamilton, Jack Haley and Joan in *George White's Scandals*, 1945.

Film Daily's review headline of the RKO picture read, "Generously produced musical offers diversion of strong popular flavor," going on to say that "Miss Davis and Haley perform with vigor" and that the film is "peppered with songs and production numbers that will capture the fancy of the man on the street." *Motion Picture Herald* thought it was an average picture, but accredited its above-normal business to Joan's popularity.

RKO reused the "Who Killed Vaudeville?" production number from this film to open their *Make Mine Laughs* feature four years later. It combined new footage with scenes from 1946's *The Bamboo Blonde* ("The Poor Little Fly on the Wall" number), "Did You Happen to Find a Heart?" from *Music in Manhattan* (1944), and other musical treats.

Make Mine Laughs, 1949.

Universal's *She Wrote the Book*, filmed from mid-January to late February and released on May 31, was the only Joan Davis film offered in 1946, but it was a corker.

She Wrote the Book, but not this one.

Though Phyllis Fowler (Gloria Stuart), wife of the Dean (John Litel) of Croyden College in Great Falls, Indiana, has authored the bestselling steamer *Always Lulu*, the Dean wants no part of his name being associated with the ignominious tome and forbids his wife to collect the $80,000 royalty check awaiting her in New York. Professor of mathematics Jane Featherstone (Joan Davis) agrees to grab the loot, but Lulu's publisher George Dixon (Lewis L. Russell) and his ad executive Jerry Marlowe (Jack Oakie) surprise the wouldn't-be author with plenty of newspaper photos and publicity. At least she gets to meet Texas engineer Eddie Caldwell (Kirby Grant) before getting conked on the head and led to believe that she really *is* author Lulu. Still, she admits at a press conference that she has no plans for a sequel to the book, so Jerry hires Joe (Mischa Auer) to play up to Lulu as Count Boris, while shipping magnate Horace Van Cleve (Thurston Hall) begins to spend Jane's/Lulu's loot as fast as she gets it from Dixon. When Eddie finds out the "truth" of Lulu's profession, he calls the relationship quits before it's started, so Joe steps in to propose marriage. He flits away fleetly after knowing she's actually broke. To save her crumbling college from ruin (and having a job to return to) once she's regained her memory, Jane invades Van Cleve's party as Lulu and causes a scandal when he spanks the annoying woman. Fearing that the scene is going to get him in trouble, Van Cleve relents to giving a large wad of dough to save the school, letting Jane quickly fly back home, with Eddie tagging along for a happy ending.

Variety claimed that the film was a satire on publishers' tricky way of using anti-publicity for banned books, such as *Forever Amber* by Kathleen Winsor, to sell yet more books. *The New York Herald Tribune* didn't care *why* the film was made, they just loved that Joan: "She departs from her usual energetic face-twisting style and plays this role almost straight, exhibiting within the limits of the material a talent for more subtle comedy performances than she usually gives." *Film Daily* called it "a very clever satire on a very 'hot' book and its very female author; destined for good grosses. Joan delivers a remarkably fine job in a dual personality role that tests the comedienne's versatility." *Motion Picture Herald*'s usual report on the box office draw was: "The weather was so extremely hot that business was poor, but those who came had good comments for the picture. Very entertaining for the local and rural patrons [in Middlebury, Vermont]." In Rochester, NY the same publication proclaimed that it "did okay Friday, but adverse word-of-mouth comments hurt Saturday's business. All in all, this was pretty dull here." And in Terre Haute, Indiana: "As a rule, Joan Davis is a good attraction in our theater, but she failed miserably in this one. It is evidently not the kind of a picture her fans expect to see her in. They stayed away in large numbers, giving us one of the worst Sunday and Monday grosses in years."

Joan made likewise headlines in the radio biz, by clashing with CBS about a giveaway she wanted to perpetuate on her series. Columbia was against it (since the Federal Communications Commission was against games of chance), preferring contests of merit, requiring skill, but that didn't stop her. She and Si wanted to slip five lucky one-dollar bills into circulation throughout the United States (Boston was one target), which would lead to prizes, with no warning which little town or large city would have the honor. Si and "the boys" (writers) constructed seven connecting scripts with contest excitement injected into them. Unfortunately, CBS got wind of it and chucked everything, causing a mad scramble on the first weekend before Monday's show to write a new script.

Perhaps this conflict was one of the reasons Swan Soap stopped sponsoring her show in June. CBS reported that her 1947 series would be run on the "cooperative-sponsor" system, which already included the likes of *America's Town Meeting of the Air* and *Information, Please*. Under the cooperative setup, the network bankrolled the show, charging each station according to its potential audience; the station in turn resold the show to local sponsors with blank spots for their commercials. In 1947, Joan had 15 different sponsors on 15 different stations. CBS hoped the number of sponsors would soon increase to 165. Under this new system, Joan made about $10,000 a week, out of which she had to pay her cast and writers.

Even with studio (and sometimes sponsor) problems, her current popularity as Queen of Comedy and articles like this in *Variety* (October 9, 1946) kept her in radio's demand. "If her stable of writers doesn't let her down, she'll be up there in the high Hoopers [ratings] before the season's over. Much of the dark talk about Miss Davis stems from the well-authenticated reports that the Lever Bros. think she's too expensive a package and would like to drop her. That's strictly the bankroller's business. But showmanwise, Miss Davis is as good as anything on the air—no, that's not much of a compliment this year; she's really much better than most."

To celebrate Joan's five-year reign as radio's Queen of Comedy, ex-husband Si took out a full-page ad in *Daily Variety* which read, "You've been my queen for 15 years."

While some magazine articles at the time were no more than fictionalized press releases aimed to throb hearts or pitch woo and current films, there was often truth behind the type. The September 29, 1947 issue of *The Hollywood Reporter* carried an article written by Joan called "This Business of Being Funny," which was probably taken from a phone interview with the star:

"Laugh and the world laughs with you is as well worn a phrase as one could dream up, but its importance to the entertainer is one of vital concern.

"Yet, every now and then someone asks me a perplexing question: 'Exactly what makes an audience laugh?'

"I wish that my good friend and co-star, Eddie Cantor, who has given so many rich years to the business of making people laugh, could answer this for me.

"Or, perchance, even my young daughter, who appeared with me in *George White's Scandals*, and who has been with me many times on my radio show, could better answer this question.

"I try out all my radio jokes on Beverly. When she likes them she okays them heartily. When she doesn't like them she says: 'Mother, maybe you had better save that joke for the Cantor picture!'

"If I'm lucky enough to be classified as humorous at times, Beverly is even funnier—she is a perfect mimic. In fact, as I once told a producer who wanted to hire her to do an impersonation of myself: 'She does everything I do—only cheaper!'

"But, now, back to the question: 'What makes people laugh?' I understand this is a problem which has baffled showmen from Florenz Ziegfeld downwards—or, to quote Eddie Cantor, upwards, according to your height.

"When I questioned Eddie further about this subject, he mentioned something he had read—an essay on laughter—that someone had written way back in the 'middling-evil' days. I realized then that Cantor was intelligent, even though he doesn't seem to mind sharing star billing with comediennes. But, because I didn't understand it, I quickly changed the subject and tried to tell him something that once made me laugh: the time I went to the circus with daughter Beverly and the guard caught her looking through a hole in the canvas.

"'Shame on you, young lady,' said the guard jokingly. 'What would your mother say if she caught you peeking like that?'

"'Ask her,' quipped my young hopeful, without moving her eyes from the hole in the canvas. 'She's right beside me at the next hole!'

"Well, we laughed over this for quite a while and then got a little intense trying to explain to each other exactly what laughter is . . . what is the basic element of laughter?

"A man doing a posterior fall on a banana peel, we decided, was hysterically funny to some people, but we concluded rather complacently that it took a little more than a banana peel to get a laugh out of us, although Heaven knows, we've done enough of them in films and on the stage ourselves.

"Then Eddie went high-brow on me again and mentioned another quotation from a book by a gentleman named Henri Gergson in his tome called *Laughter*, in which he pointed out that 'some philosophers had defined man as an animal which laughs.'

"Having always thought that Henri was Charles Chaplin's late pal, who used to run Henri's restaurant up on Hollywood Boulevard, I didn't quite get it until Eddie told me an animal story. He took a few liberties with it, but it went something like this: It was about a woman who took a large chimpanzee in a wheelchair to see Eddie's film version of his Broadway hit, **Kid Boots**.

"When the usher refused her admission with such a companion, she said indignantly, 'Well, he'll be terribly disappointed, because he LOVED the play!'"

"Then we decided that perhaps we laugh at stupidities and frailties of people we see on the stage or screen, because, subconsciously, we identify ourselves with the characters we are watching.

"We were on our third cup of tea down at the studio commissary by the time we had threshed this out, when Eddie suddenly stumped me with: 'Joan, how do YOU make people laugh?'"

"Then, I remembered the innumerable times when, although I had been weighed down with funny hats and clothes, and did those posterior falls, the audience hadn't laughed. I remembered also the day when I was about seven, wearing pigtails and looking very much like Beverly did at seven and making my first stage appearance in my home town of St. Paul, Minnesota. The audience, as I remember, howled with laughter over my serious dramatic efforts, and I left the stage in tears—I've been a comedienne ever since.

Joan and Dorothy Lamour on radio's *Variety Theatre*, 1949.

"My memories were suddenly and rudely disturbed by an incident. There was a crash of dishes and a cry. Everyone looked in the direction of the noise which came from right behind me. A nice waitress, her face red with embarrassment, was standing motionless over the victim of her accident. Yes, it was me with a cascade of red, sticky fluid, all over my nice blue suit, and the look of shock on my face must have been incredibly funny.

"'It's catsup, ma'am!' the waitress said in a terrified voice. 'They make it with tomatoes!' Then she dashed back to the kitchen.

"'See what I mean!' roared Eddie Cantor. And I did—and started laughing at myself.

"So, near the conclusion of this article, I still do not know the secret of comedy. Laughter is an extremely elusive muse, and wooing it in terms universally comprehended is not an easy matter. But over the years we have come to learn the basic elements that motivate all humor, and properly served up and adorned, these elements cannot fail to provide good comedy.

"What constitutes comedy cannot be set down in any academic discussion. Situations, dialogue, delivery, slapstick, players, all the human elements have their part in the finished product. And assembling them in the proper proportions is the particular forte of the comedy technician.

"This I do know—I have encountered no more human urge more universal or more eagerly desirous of fulfillment than the will to laugh. Now, more than ever, the world has earned the right to laugh. With the trials and tribulations, the care and heartaches of the war years behind us, the feeling for release from mood and problems makes comedy the all-important entertainment goal, both here and abroad. The desire to laugh knows no geographical bounds, surmounts every barrier of race, color and creed. It is the universal language if ever there was one. Apart from its commercial aspects, it is easily apparent what a power for disseminating goodwill and good fellowship infectious laughter can be.

"Speaking of mattresses, some people say it's nice to reach for a pillow as you fall. All I can say is, you'd have to have the services of both a valet and a prophet.

"But with my system, you can now walk in the dark unscathed, afraid no longer of the kid's toys, your wife's broom or furniture on wheels. Me, I always carry a flashlight, I like to see where I'm falling."

Roots were also important to the development of a comedic personality. She expanded her explanation of comedy to other reporters: "Most of the good comedians on the screen today started out in vaudeville. And I think that's the only way in which one may learn the important business of timing one's act to get the best laugh return. After you'd been on the vaudeville circuit grind for a couple of years, facing all sorts of audiences, you developed a 'feel' for the comedy situations that carried you through."

But for all the slapstick and squeaky voice shtick, offstage, Joan was able to show off her eye for glamour. She was usually considered one of the best-dressed people in Hollywood by the press. Contrary to her man-chasing, plain-looking screen persona, Joan had a nice figure and an inherent sense of style that kept her more than pleased to dress up for a night on the town. Whether it was a Friday evening's boxing (as a spectator, of course) at the American Legion Stadium, or going to the country club to swim or play golf, she wanted the public to (rightly) know that she was more than just a self-slap in the face.

Of course, appearing in public against her screen persona wasn't always a good thing. She once gave an interview as her usual shy, retiring self in a gray, smartly-tailored suit and stunningly groomed blonde hair. When accused of putting on an act for the reporter, she seriously replied, "Why should I have to put on an act for you? You're not booking anything."

Chapter 10

Love In Doom

Nineteen Forty-seven was a tough year: no film roles, a busy radio schedule, and a marriage that just wasn't working. She would divorce Si on December 8, 1948. Another source claimed that Joan sued him for divorce on November 3, 1947, being granted on December 1, 1947. She obtained the divorce from Superior Judge Thurmond Clarke, via a "default divorce," citing, "my husband refused to take me out to places of entertainment. When friends came to visit us, he went upstairs to bed, ignoring me and them. He also stayed out nights and told me when he came back in the early morning hours he had been 'fishing' or 'hunting.'" Her attorney, Sylvan Covey, told the court Joan and Si agreed to divide the custody of 14-year-old Beverly and that no alimony was sought. Property matters and the sharing of Bev's custody had been settled out of court previously. Wills did not contest the divorce. The couple had been separated since October 1. More than likely the pressure of being a backstage husband continued to drive a wedge between once equal egos.

Only a few days later the papers reported the blossoming romance between Joan and Danny Elman, president of the Chicago-Fort Dearborn Lumber Company. It was strongly rumored that they would marry when her divorce was final. Gossip columnist Louella O. Parsons had her number, though, when she wrote in the *Los Angeles Examiner* on January 27, 1948, "Don't hold your breath until Joan Davis marries Elman, wealthy Chicago lumberman. I'm not going to hold mine. Although the engagement was given to me bona fide, I have a hunch the wedding bells will never ring for the comedienne and her 'fiancé.' I happen to know that Joan, and a man she has liked for a long time, had a tiff—and we girls are given to moments of pique in circumstances like this. Recently, she has been seen dining frequently—usually at the Kings—with Jack Melvin, but he isn't the man I mean." Louella was right about the bells.

News reports indicated a spot of trouble at least as late as July of that year, citing that Joan wanted to wait until her divorce was final before setting a wedding date. Besides, she and Si were still "good friends," occasionally dining together in the public eye. And on January 5, 1949, Joan told reporter Harrison Carroll that, after thinking it over, she and Danny decided not to rush into marriage. "We may even wait a year," she said, preferring (as always) to concentrate on work.

According to Beverly's ex-husband Lee Bamber, "I worked for her boyfriend Danny a short while at his manufacturing plant in downtown Los Angeles. He was a short pudgy Jewish fellow. He lived with Joan but was kicked out of the house a good share of the time to stay in a condo up on Sunset Blvd. Bev always said she just kept him around to have a whipping boy."

To keep things peachy in the public eye, Joan's radio sponsor thought it would be a nice idea to have daughter Beverly write (or ghostwrite) a sweet piece on the happy Davis home in *Radio Mirror* for Mother's Day. It gave a peppy overview of Joan's career and a rare glimpse into some of the more private corners of their life together. "My Mother" began:

"When my friends and I are listening to Mother's program on CBS on Saturday nights, hearing her talk in that funny, cracked falsetto, or when we go to the movies and see her doing her comedy falls on the screen, someone's sure to ask, 'Is Joan Davis really like that—at home, I mean?'

"Well, I couldn't say no and I couldn't say yes. Being a fifteen-year-old daughter who thinks that her mother is just about tops in the mother department, I'm prejudiced. Maybe the best thing to do is to tell you about her, and let you judge for yourself what I mean when I say that I can't make a definite yes or no answer to that question!

"Most of the time, Mother certainly doesn't look the part of the Joan Davis of radio or movies. In person she's slim and sort of elegant, where she looks angular and thin when you see her in a picture or in front of the microphone. She's very pretty—and yet she's always made up to look unattractive for her parts. At home she's graceful, where she's all jutting elbows and flying legs in her Joan Davis character.

"But when at home there's something about her that is still Joan Davis, as you know her. She thinks of something funny, and that sly, oh-yeah look comes into her eyes and her voice cracks in the middle and when she tells the story she has to do it with gestures. Her humor is a very real part of her.

"Maybe I can give you an example of the way her humor works in with the rest of her.

"She collects antiques. I'll tell you more about them later. But one of her prize possessions is a charming blue-and-white-and-rose, hand-painted with delicate figures, English porcelain *spittoon*! There it sits in our Bel-Air house, in our living room with all the fine, expensive furniture she has collected over the years, right next to an elegant wingback chair. That's my mother. That's Joan Davis.

"As she says: 'What'll I do if someone ever really spits in it?'

"Do you see what I mean?

"Not that she spends all her time being funny—the major portion of it, at home, belongs to me, and to her job of being my mother.

"She always makes me face what *might* happen. She always starts off with 'Yes—but, Beverly, what would you do if . . . ?' And it's good for me. She's giving me balance.

"Mother was helping me rehearse a speech I had to give in school. I made a slip of the tongue. Nothing serious. I started to go on as if it hadn't happened.

"But she stopped me.

"'What would you do if that should happen when you're facing that whole roomful of kids? What if someone laughs at you? What if the teacher stops you? What would you do, Beverly?'

"I still wasn't taking it seriously.

"'Oh, I'd just say my braces slipped and I'd better get 'em fixed.'

"'But that's good! That way they won't be embarrassed for you. You remember to make a joke out of your own mistakes and you'll have people on your side—laughing with you.'

"So *what would you do, Beverly—if* has become something I can expect from my mother. Something I know I'm lucky to get from an expert like Joan Davis. She's always approved my wanting to be a comedienne—though the story I've heard is that the first word I said as a baby was 'Mama,' only I said it in that same funny falsetto voice she uses on the stage. And I understand she gave my father one horrified look and gasped—'Oh, no! We've got another comic!'

"Especially in radio you have to be prepared to take what comes and think fast—be ready to slip in an impromptu gag if the one you've just read falls flat. Or pick up a fluff you've made or someone else has made and turn it into a joke on yourself. This, I think, is one of my mother's biggest talents. It's one of the things that has made her a star in her own right.

"Also her quality of independence. She never wanted to be just one half of a team. She wanted to be able to carry an act by herself. To do this she has developed a kind of special comedy personality that works well with other people, but doesn't necessarily need a steady partner—or any partner at all.

She fits into all kinds of movies, wherever they have an opportunity to let her be herself.

"Certain kinds of roles just become naturals—they are 'Joan Davis' roles. That's why she's done so many pictures, I guess. I saw *Sweetheart of the Fleet* and *Two Latins from Manhattan* that she made for Columbia, a dozen times at least. And I spent most of my allowance in motion picture houses when she appeared with Kay Kyser in RKO's *Around the World* and for her latest one, *If You Knew Susie*, with Eddie Cantor.

"I've seen them all—these and many others. But I go not only because she's my mother and I think she's a great comedienne. I go because I want to study why she is so funny—what makes her a star. It's like a sixth sense, I know, but I try to figure out what goes into it.

"Maybe it's because she works so hard at it. That part an audience doesn't know—it seems so easy, standing up there cracking jokes and taking the laughs on herself. It must seem a natural to her to get herself into funny situations and out of them. In radio she doesn't use the slapstick to get the laughs. Here her mastery of the quick-punch gag line has put her up on top. It's what has earned her the title of Queen of Comedy.

"The only time I've seen her absolutely speechless-not able to even make a wisecrack—was when the college students of America chose her as the 'First Lady of Laughter.' It was a poll made by three hundred and seventeen college newspapers. She was so pleased!

"Working takes up a lot of her time, and now she can't even seem to get a day off to play the golf she likes so much. Sometimes we slip off together and go fishing off the pier at Malibu Beach—she was with me the day I caught the barracuda!

"When Mother isn't working she's resting. As the saying goes, she 'knocks herself out' every time she does a broadcast or a picture. And when she isn't resting she likes to see people. Me, I think I have a little edge on all her other friends. It isn't often that mothers and daughters enjoy each other's company as much as they do friends of their own age. We do.

"Mother enjoys reading. I get enough of that in school. Especially since I'm trying to get all A's on my report cards. Mother thinks it's because I've been promised a convertible car when I graduate if I can keep up the good work—but actually it's because I've just got to beat her record. She got *all* A's when she was in school!

"About the only time we disagree is over Mister. Mother likes dogs but she swears Mister is no dog—he's an elephant. He isn't very big, really. He's a Kerry-Blue puppy and I'm training him to be a champion. Mother says, 'Just train him. Period.' But I think he has very good manners. He just gets excited sometimes and he likes people so much he can't help jumping all over them and wanting to kiss their faces and he likes to pretend he's a lap dog. But I got her point. It's Mister versus the crockery.

Teaching an old dog new nothing.

"Mother has spent years collecting her lovely, priceless antique Dresden figurines and her fine Englishware (she has names for it but I never can remember) and the cranberry glasses. Mister, let loose in the living room, is really a hazard. Once he toppled a gold-and-mirror fan she had just found and just placed on the end table. Fortunately there was no damage done. It didn't break.

"But if he ever breaks the little miniature rocking chair that my grandfather carved for Mother—oh, dear!

"She has very good taste. She designed and decorated our whole house—and even had a three-room playhouse built onto it, just for me. That was a wonderful place when I was growing up. I could entertain in it and study in it and play house in it. But it seems a little childish, now that I'm fifteen, and I very seldom use it.

"In fact, I'm old enough now so that we can wear each other's clothes. I borrow hers and she grabs a sweater of mine, once in a while. But there's a limit to sharing . . . I got a gorgeous make-up and dressing case for my birthday and—do you know—I have to keep the combination lock a secret from her, to keep her out of it?

"She's an awful problem to me, sometimes.

"I almost weakened and let her into it, once. She was so good about helping me with my homework. But after the last time, I decided it wasn't worth it.

"My teacher at school told us we were to write an essay about anything we chose. It took me a little while to think of something, but finally one evening when Mother and I were sitting in front of our new television set at home, it struck me that that would be a fine subject. Television.

"So I got out my notebook and went to work. I struggled with it and at last had it done—all but the punch line, the ending. (Being Joan Davis' daughter has made me conscious of punch lines and things like that.) I needed a final poetic touch to round out the essay. But I couldn't think of a thing.

"Mother had been sort of coaching from the sidelines all this time-though I must say her help consisted mostly of thinking of all the crazy, fantastical things you could say about television. Though not in a school essay. And making faces at me—breaking me up—just when I was working my darndest.

"But now she volunteered to help. She'd think of something poetic.

"'I've got it!' she said, seriously. 'Look at the rose in the vase on top of the television cabinet. Why don't you link the two together—the miracle of television and the rose. The miracle and the rose!'

"That was it. That was my punch line. The miracle and the rose.

"So what happened—? I guess my teacher didn't think much of Mother's poetical flights, because she wrote across it—'And isn't a rose a miracle, too?'

"I decided the homework help wasn't worth giving Mother the combination to my make-up kit. Instead, I'm teaching her to jitterbug. She's a wonderful dancer and she likes to go to nightclubs so she can rumba. But she's still not hep to the jive—and, believe me, the movie studios would pay good money to put on the screen the contortions we go through as she and I clear the living room so she can practice the jitterbug.

"It's really fun to be Joan Davis' daughter.

"Like any other mother she supervises my clothes, watches that I don't use too much lipstick, knows all about my health, takes me to the dentist and consoles me for having to wear braces on my teeth just now. Some of the most beautiful actresses, she tells me (and a comedienne doesn't have to be beautiful), wore braces on their teeth when they were younger, and that makes me feel better. She helps me with my homework (when I let her!) and likes me just as much when I'm bad as when I'm good.

"Though her radio program houses her, and the many days she has to spend on motion picture lots when she's making a movie keep her from being with me as much as we both would like, I actually get more than my share of her free time. She not only worries about my dates and my health and things like that—she has to worry about my career, too.

"Mother says that her greatest problem is keeping 'hands off.' She refused, absolutely, to coach me when I had my first honest-to-goodness—my first, and so far my only—[featured] role in a motion picture, Eagle-Lion Studios' *Mickey.* [*George White's Scandals* was her first.] She doesn't want me to be a carbon copy of Joan Davis—which certainly wouldn't be the worst thing that could happen to me! At home, life sometimes becomes a battle of seeing which of us can top the other's gags. And darn it, she always wins!

"Yes, Joan Davis is very much okay for a mother—but she seems too young and too full of pep and too much of a standout personality in herself ever to fit into the usual maternal picture. So many of my friends just seem to have their mothers for backgrounds—there if they need them, but most of the time just someone to remind them to wear their rubbers if it's raining.

"I think I'll end this story the way I used to end that act when I was five years old and on the stage with Mother—

"'I think my Mommy is the most wonderful, the greatest, the funniest comedienne in the world—isn't that what you wanted me to say, Mommy?'

"Only I believe it. And anyway, I'm too big now to get pulled off by the ear."

According to Bev's first husband, Lee Bamber, Joan wasn't so nice to her own mother, Nina. "She treated her mother just terribly. Grandmother Davis lived in this one room, one bath, and that's it for better than 15 years. Joan paid the rent and gave her a meager allowance for answering her fan mail. It was just enough to take care of basic necessities. Nina was greatly depressed having lived in that dive for so long, had no friends, no transportation, and lived just a plain old lonesome life. Bev and I included her when possible, but that wasn't very often. We started talking about finding her a more enjoyable place to live and found this apartment on Hollywood Blvd. with a daylight kitchen, everything to make her more comfortable, and for just a few dollars more. She was ecstatic, so we moved her in immediately and I went to work. It wasn't an hour later before Nina was on the phone hysterical, saying I had to move her back into the Las Palmas or Joan would stop her stipend. I tried to calm her and said I would call Joan and straighten things out, so I did, and Joan became extremely irate. I told her not to worry about the additional rent and that really sent her into a tizzy.

Joan said next time she saw me she was going to knock me on my ass. Needless to say, Joan won out and poor miserable Nina moved back to her old dismal hotel room.

Bev and Nina.

"I remember one day when we were taking Nina somewhere and we stopped so Bev could run an errand. As Bev was getting out of the car, she commented to Nina about how bad her boobs were sagging. As soon as Bev was out of sight, Nina broke out crying. She said she had no money for underclothes, that hers were all worn out. She said she just barely had money for food. I'm trying to give you a picture of how miserable a wealthy woman could treat her poor, lonely mother."

William Bast, who dated Bev for a few months in the 1950s (before leaving him for roommate James Dean), had almost exactly the same comments to make about Nina's treatment. So did Bev's ex-husband, Alan Grossman:

"Nina was such a *sweet* person. On a scale of one to ten she was a ten. She may have loved Joan, I don't know, but she had to put up with the terrible treatment because she had no money. She always wore the same dress, always dressed in black with a little purple. I'm sure she had more than one dress, but it always seemed like she was dressed the same way. What she was put through by Joan was just beyond belief. Joan had one of the few gold El Dorados, a very limited Cadillac. But Nina didn't drive. She took the bus everywhere. I'm not kidding, Nina had a one-room apartment, and Joan had this gigantic house. I didn't realize at the time what a louse Joan was. Please make sure you make people know how great the grandmother was."

Chapter 11
Running Out Of Film

1948's only Joan Davis offering was basically a duet with Eddie Cantor, in which the two were almost straight men for the incredible plot unfolding around them. *If You Knew Susie*, originally titled *Rich Man, Poor Man*, ended up being Cantor's last picture (except for a cameo in 1952's *The Story of Will Rogers*), celebrating (so newspapers said) his 38 years in show business. While it didn't have the musical and energetic bite of *Show Business*, the RKO picture energetically opened with Susie (Joan) and Sam (Eddie) Parker performing "My, How the Time Goes By" (for which RKO paid $20,000 for the rights) in blackface.

The Parkers were established vaudeville performers who have settled down in Sam's old family home in Brookford, Masschusetts with kids they hope won't follow in their prancing footsteps. They're given a hard time by their First Families of the Revolution neighbors since the Parkers are running a cheap chicken and steak restaurant in order to make ends meet. All that changes when they find a letter hidden in the wall, signed by the biggies: Washington, Jefferson, Franklin, telling of the bravery of Jonathan Parker, Sam's great-great-great-grandfather, during the Revolutionary War. Determined to prove the letter genuine, the couple hop to Washington D.C., where they're promptly given the runaround. Reporter Mike Garrett (Allyn Joslyn), up against tough times from loan sharks, offers the Parkers the use of his paper's penthouse for a hundred bucks, though he has no right to rent the place.

Not only do the Parkers finally learn that the letter is the real thing, but it seems their government owes the Parker estate 50,000 pounds sterling, with compound interest. That's more than seven billion dollars. Mike's got his story and the Parkers have more media attention than a campaigning Congressman. Of course, Congress declare the I.O.U. no good, and after a run in with Mike's gangsters, the Parkers head back home, broke and disgraced. Meantime, Congress investigates them and the Senate decides they should have the loot. For some reason, the Parkers don't want 7 billion dollars and decide to remain poor. Go figure.

Film Daily's headline proclaimed, "this Cantor-Davis romp should gayly make the big money grade; should attract big general audiences," stating further that, "producer Eddie Cantor loaded this one with everything the eventual target

Joan and Eddie black up.

demands from both himself and Joan Davis in the line of laugh getting material, a light farce story treatment, songs and the familiar-like set. Zestful is the word for the display given by Cantor and Miss Davis."

The *Los Angeles Evening Herald Express* called the picture "even better than expected. It's corny, to be sure, but if you don't howl at a lot of it and smile at the rest of it, then you are made of sterner stuff than I. Both Eddie and Joan are in rare good form. The latter in more ways than one. A lot of people are going to be surprised by Joan's pretty legs."

In the summer of 1949, single Joan now started life anew in another way. Radio's *Leave it to Joan* was first heard on CBS at 9:00 p.m., sponsored by the American Tobacco Company. She was a department store salesgirl, again chasing the men, and bringing in an impressive $8,250 weekly for her "troubles." It was to be her final radio series, ending on August 28, 1950, still written (at least partially) by the ex, Mr. Wills, and sometimes featured young Bev as Joan's sister.

The New York Herald Tribune's John Crosby, heatedly tired of the old formula coming back, wrote, "Miss Davis [is] changeless as the tides. She's still a sex-starved, addled and very, very noisy girl. It's been the standard comedy role for women since the days of Mack Sennett and Miss Davis is not a girl to rough up tradition. As a matter of fact, Miss Davis started her film work with Mack Sennett, an experience that left permanent scars.

"Much of her new show smells faintly of lavender and Mack Sennett. As a department store employee, Miss Davis messes up private enterprise with such diligence, she could easily be investigated by a Senate Committee.

"The jokes concerning Miss Davis's difficulties in catching a man have been honed to such a fine point it's almost a mathematical exercise thinking up new ones. This has produced what might be described as the inevitable joke. You know what's coming, but you don't know exactly when it's going to get there."

A typical gag, he wrote, went as follows:

DEPT. STORE MANAGER:	Thought you'd do well in ladies' dresses.
JOAN:	I haven't done too well in them so far.
MGR:	What color is your hair?
JOAN:	On top, or at the roots?
MGR:	I'll put you in the exchange department. I can't think what harm you'll do there.
JOAN:	I'll think of something.
MGR:	I've never been so insulted in my life.
JOAN:	Oh, you *must* have been.

The review concluded: "As I recall, the old Joan Davis show once had more plot than *Gone with the Wind* and it seemed a wonder they could work it all in, in half an hour. Being a summer show though—it's picked up a sponsor and will continue through the winter—*Leave it to Joan* seems predicated on the assumption a man might want to drop out to the icebox for a beer without falling hopelessly behind. Somewhere Miss Davis has rounded up the most responsive [studio] audience around."

Back on the film front . . .

Traveling Saleswoman (1950) isn't the funniest Davis vehicle either, but it has gas in it. Joan plays eager Mabel King, who is sure of two things in life: the power of her father's (Harry Hayden) King Soap and the marriageability of boyfriend Waldo (Andy Devine), one of the worst salesmen on the road. Knowing that the bank won't lend them enough to get out of debt and truly establish the greatness of King Soap, Mabel takes to the trail herself to scrounge up enough orders to interest banker Chumhil (Charles Halton) in refinancing them. Waldo doesn't believe a woman's place is on the road, so follows her, unknowingly becoming involved in a rumor that a store owner, who can't get rid of all the King Soap he bought long ago, started which states that a diamond ring was lost in one of the boxes as it was packaged. Mabel hears of this and buys all the boxes herself. Luckily, she also runs into an itchy-scalp Indian who loses his scratch after a King Soap treatment and saves the day for Mabel at the end when all the Indians (plus the nearby townsfolk who gratefully order King Soap when Mabel thwarts the Indian uprising through kindness) promise to use only King. The Kings stock their factory with a generous supply of Indians, finally kicking the soap factory into top speed.

A hard sell for *Traveling Saleswoman*, 1950.

The *Los Angeles Examiner* reported that Joan went on a two-week stint as a real door-to-door sales girl to prep for the role, though that's a bit hard to swallow. *The New York Herald Tribune* cautiously stated that "Miss Davis is too much of a craftsman not to wring a few bits of humor out of a series of loosely connected situations that would be of dubious value even on radio." The film failed to wow the general public; even though Joan received more than 2,000 letters from fans in her hometown of Minneapolis requesting a special premiere of her first indie picture.

Production only took 15 days on this one, from August 5 to August 20, 1949, released on the following 5th of January. At the end of filming, Joan's then-beau Danny Elman gave her a diamond bracelet to celebrate her first stint as an independent film producer. Newspapers kept announcing the impending marriage of the long-standing couple, but by the end of the December 1949, reports were fading away.

Then came two more nothing roles.

Love That Brute in 1950 remade Fox's 1941 film, *Tall, Dark and Handsome,* and starred Paul Douglas as Big Ed Hanley, a gangster of the 1920s who falls for classy governess Ruth Manning (Jean Peters) and casts a few kids—and dancer Mamie Sage (Joan Davis) as housekeeper—in order to keep her around. Of course, she wants him to go straight, but it takes a lot of doing.

Based on the novel *Legal Bride* by Robert Carson and filmed between early July and late August 1950, *The Groom Wore Spurs* (1952) put Joan far, far

Joan keeps it clean in *Traveling Saleswoman*, 1950.

behind stars Ginger Rogers and Jack Carson, even with third billing, as Ginger's roommate.

Lawyer A.J. Furnival (Rogers) meets her heartthrob movie cowboy, Wild Ben

With Ginger Rogers in *The Groom Wore Spurs*, 1952.

Castle (Carson), to do some legal work for him, only to discover he's as far removed from a cowboy as an astronaut. Still, she's smitten enough to fall for the lug's marriage proposal, then realizes that he probably married her because of her name, which erased a large debt Castle had with a certain mobster, Harry Kallen (Stanley Ridges), who happened to be a friend of A.J.'s father. She decides to make a man of him, though it's tough going, especially after he's accused of Kallen's murder. After a harrowing, crashing plane ride with the killer, Castle finally redeems himself in A.J.'s eyes by roping the rascal with a rope trick from one of his films, and kisses his wife passionately in front of the arriving press.

The *New York Herald Tribune* was sympathetic to Joan, who only had a couple scenes, stating: "Trying to squeeze a laugh from worn-out material is too tough for a comic." Perhaps taking small roles this late in her life is what prompted Joan to take the plunge into television the following year.

Guy-stalking Susie Skubblegrave (Joan Davis) was up against a lot of competition as a *Harem Girl* (1952), a Columbia Picture, which began shooting near the end of October, released the following February.

In search of something sweeter than a boring candy store life in Cedar Rapids, Susie boards a cruise where she follows Princess Shareen (Peggie Castle) to the small town of All Bazzar as her traveling companion. There she disguises herself

Joan and Peggie Castle in *Harem Girl*, 1952.

as the Princess so that she can meet Majeed (Paul Marion) in the desert so they can plot the overthrow of the evil Jamal (Donald Randolph), who has been running and ruining her country since the death of the Princess' dear father, Sheik Fared. Shareen intends to rescue her friend, though her rebellious supporters have no guns with which to storm the palace. Dancing like a rhythm-less ostrich, Susie manages to snag the keys to the gun stash during a harem girl entertainment, finally jumping into a vegetable cart to avoid capture.

Susie has heard that the guns are hidden somewhere in El Haroon and, in true *Hold That Ghost* fashion, is scared sheik-less as she finds the entrance to the guns in a dark cave among Jamal's creeping assassins. Alas, the guns literally weigh a ton, so Susie dashes back to the palace to delay the forced wedding between Hassan (Jamal's representative) and Shareen until armed help can arrive. Susie manages to organize the first-ever sit-down strike among the harem dancing girls: they refuse to dance for the wedding. Jamal fumes and calls in the guards, who are unfortunately all the boyfriends of the strikers. A fight breaks out between the palace guards and the soldiers, with Susie frantically collecting up rifles to show the townsmen that the guns *have* arrived. This causes the townsmen to rush Jamal's army and hand him over to the better late than never French Foreign Legion, which hands Susie over a fat check for capturing Jamal. Of course, the true prize is hearing about the Legion; seems the ideal place for a woman on the make . . . she marches right out with them.

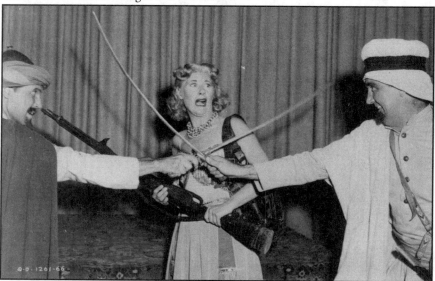

Shoot someone, *Harem Girl!*

One review was a carbon of her previous film: "Miss Davis milks a few laughs and does as best she can with poor material." The Arabian adventure turned out to be Joan's swan song on the silver screen (not counting a few compilation films containing old scenes) before the manic star got her man and turned to full-time television. It was an unfortunate film to end with. But television *was* calling.

Chapter 12
Jim Married Joan

Television was king in 1950. Radio was a lost nephew, powerless, and whimpering on an allowance. Every name in show business knew it, and Joan Davis was more astute than the average radio actress. Most comedians who began in the very early years of TV, often copied their radio format exactly. Being unsure precisely how to crack the back of a new medium, they prefer to lean on the tried-and-true formula of their joke making. Joan's first attempt was no different. But she quickly learned.

In 1950, two years before her regular series began, she made a pilot named *Let's Join Joanie*, which basically took up where her radio series left off, with Joan as a hat salesgirl in a shop called Hats by Anatole. Again, she was constantly man-hungry; this time, for Jim Benson, joining a health club just because he preferred his women husky. Joe Kearns (Mr. Wilson from *Dennis the Menace*) played Anatole, though Joan was the only name on the credits. The old formula failed to attract a sponsor, and the pilot went unsold, though it was aired on January 12, 1951.

She knew she needed a new gimmick for a new audience, and brainstormed with Si to come up with something more family oriented, to fit in with the current crop of homogenized entertainment. In early 1952, Joan recorded a television pilot called *I Married Joan* at General Service Studios in Hollywood, and by October 15, 1952, it had a time slot with NBC at 8-8:30 p.m., Wednesdays, for sponsor General Electric. From the start, she was determined to remain in charge of her new medium. Not only did she retain rights to the show, but she paid herself a weekly salary of $7,500 and had ex-hubby Si writing (often uncredited) for it. Joan insisted on producing the show herself via Joan Davis Productions. (She was already investing; she owned a healthy piece of the Ord system, which made 3-D movies.)

The formula decided upon was inspired slapstick to draw in and whack the viewer over the head, with half an hour of Lucille Ball-like verve and Joan Davis-like manic pratfalls and dexterous klutzing. Only this time she was falling over a man she already *had*. She was the wife of Judge Bradley Stevens, who had married this whirling scatterbrain because she keeps him in stitches, sometimes literally. She was a childless housewife who could ruin the house,

He married Joan.

the furniture, demolish her husband's chances at reformation work and domestic normalcy; besides optional weird schemes including buying a moose head at an auction, thinking she's allergic to Brad after a plethora of sneezes, hiding money in a shotgun, learning acrobatics, and renting the house thinking Brad has been drafted. It also delved into plots that *I Love Lucy* could never get into, such as the time Joan winds up in traffic court presided over by guess who? After sentencing she then proceeds to make Brad's life a living hell.

The new pilot, written by Arthur Stander & Phil Sharp and directed by Bickersons creator Phil Rapp, was exactly what NBC was looking for. It began its 3-year, 39-episode journey on October 15, 1952 and wowed audiences immediately.

Every show began with the catchy, very '50s theme song (written by Richard Mack), doo-doo-doo'ed (like a train) by the Robert Shaw Chorale, after a thumb rings the doorbell (chiming the start of the song) on the sweet little Stevens house.

I MARRIED JOAN
WHAT A GIRL, WHAT A WHIRL, WHAT A LIFE!
OH . . . I MARRIED JOAN
WHAT A MIND, LOVE IS BLIND, WHAT A WIFE!
GIDDY AND GAY, ALL DAY SHE KEEPS MY HEART LAUGHIN'
NEVER KNOW WHERE HER BRAIN HAS FLOWN
TO EACH HIS OWN
CAN'T DENY THAT'S WHY I MARRIED JOAN!

Over the song, there's a close-up of the perfect wedding cake, with an almost sickly-sweet smiling Joan standing before it, still in pristine wedding gown. Joan was obviously pitched as the star, even with the announcer, while poor Jim Backus (Judge Bradley Stevens) received a "with" credit on the final screen.

The premiere episode was the only real set-up to the series: trying to placate a couple arguing over a fur coat, Judge Bradley relates his own story of a fur coat causing trouble in his life, back when Joan was an airline hostess.

Variety's review of the show opener was enthusiastic, especially since she finally *had* her man and was no longer constricted in a store environment: "Miss Davis mates herself easily to the medium, moves in gracefully as if nothing has changed. The plain fact is that very little has, considering her video baptism is on film. She is no less the fine mugger and cutup who wastes little motion getting down to brash tacks. She retains her sensitive ear and eye for the ridiculous and is a tongue-in-cheeker of unusual deftness." The only thing the reviewer wasn't sure of was "whether Miss Davis should solo the end plug" for the sponsor. The formula certainly worked well enough to interest the network in a whole first season.

The change felt good, as Joan told *The New York Times*: "It's the first time I've ever done a domestic comedy. But since I made a reputation as a physical comedienne, I had to continue. We feel that the script is adult, but we don't want to disappoint the children in the audience. There are lots of them from three-year-olds and up."

Behind the scenes with *I Married Joan*.

It wasn't necessarily a happy time for co-star Jim Backus.

When he began the *I Married Joan* chapter of his autobiography, ***Forgive Us Our Digressions*** (written with his wife Henny), he admitted that "trying to be a friend of Joan Davis's was like watching your mother-in-law go over a cliff in your brand-new Rolls." Some of the stories he told give a surprising and often nasty picture of Joan the businesswoman. Such as the time she grudgingly agreed to having cocktails with the sponsors' wives in Joan's Bel-Air home, only after G.E. promised to redo her kitchen with the latest appliances and to air condition her entire house. As Backus wrote, "A much softened Joan agreed. 'But only an hour!' she snarled. This was just dandy with the NBC executives, as they well knew—as we all did—that Joan had a three-drink tolerance. One drop over that and she lashed out at the nearest target like a crazed asp." Unfortunately, after a third drink, Joan's joking ways insulted one of the ladies, and her kitchen stayed the same.

Joan in the kitchen.

Writing about her own experiences with Joan in the same book, Henny Backus, who played Joan's girlfriend Harriet on the series, basically agreed with her husband that "professionally I found her to be warm, talented, and giving. Socially, although we were constantly thrown together, we had very little to say to each other."

Lee Bamber's memories of Joan at this time weren't pleasant either: "The show was Joan's baby lock, stock and barrel—controlled it like a dictator. She was paid X number of dollars per episode and all expenses were hers. The cheaper she could produce an episode, the more she netted. I can't remember what Bev was paid but it wasn't startling. Very good money for a 20-year-old, but not enough to be able to go out and buy a house.

"Joan created a lot of petty jealousy. She would get people competing for her attention and approval, so there was constant backstabbing and trickery going on for Joan's attention. There was one young girl, I would swear it was Cathy Bates but I can't be sure, that was constantly trying to shoot Beverly down. Normally you wouldn't think it was very smart to try and shoot the star's daughter down, but Joan just relished in it and encouraged it."

It wasn't all pain, however, as both Backus and Joan liked to joke a lot. Knowing that Joan was already too wealthy to buy Christmas presents for, Jim hit upon the snazzy idea of posing for a cheesecake photo every year. The first Christmas, he dressed in stockings and a Marlene Dietrich wig; the next—boots, cowboy hat and holster covering his "gun"; the third year, "I turned my nude back to the camera and provocatively dropped a silver fox over my lower cleavage." They were perfect for Joan, who proudly displayed them on top of her piano, along with her pictures of Ike, Bishop Sheen and Sister Kenny. (When Joan's house burned down in 1963, Backus received some very weird looks from the firemen who were dragging out the furniture, piano included.)

Backus considered the three *IMJ* years quite an ordeal and lamented the fact that every show's script, which ran 55 pages, had to be memorized rather than the more popular form of reading from TelePromTers or idiot cards, since *IMJ* was more fast-paced and physical. "This means," wrote Jim, "that in three years I memorized approximately 6,545 pages of dialogue, which is equivalent to memorizing *War and Peace* and *Gone With the Wind*." Both he and Joan were dubious about being able to do it, but things got easier after the first few months, especially for Joan whom Jim considered to have a photographic memory.

Joan began memorizing her script on Wednesday night, rehearsed it Thursday and was ready to go in front of the cameras all day Friday; often from eight in the morning until 8:00 or 12:30 at night. Joan admitted, "I'd rather shoot it in one day and get it over with. I work like a dog. We use three cameras shooting simultaneously on every scene. When I take a pratfall, we've got it from three different angles and I don't have to do it over again. We never reshoot anything. There isn't time."

She told Jack Gaver of *United Press*, "I practically live at the Hollywood studio where our shows are filmed. I even sleep there on Thursday nights instead of driving to my home, which is only 30 minutes away."

The show had the best scriptwriters available to early television, many of which made their mark in entertainment history: Neil Simon, Sherwood Schwartz, Abe Burrows. She called all of her writers "boys" and had an uncanny ability to add on zingers or tags to scenes or gags, which Backus called "nothing short of miraculous." He was highly complimentary toward her education in vaudeville, even if he didn't find her particularly bright outside the realm of show business or even comedy. But her sense of comedy construction—even knowing what word to shave off a line so the rhythm of the gag would play best—was on par with Jack Benny's writers.

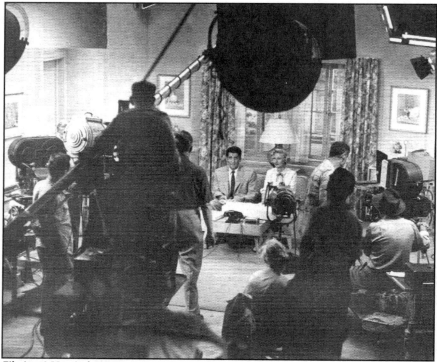

Filming *I Married Joan*.

According to Joan, via Backus, "pickles" sounded funny, while "relish" did not—"seven" could get howls while "six" laid an egg—and no one would move to "Cleveland" when "Pittsburgh" got the belly laughs. Joan knew every joke ever written and the laws and tag lines that governed them. Working together with her for thirteen hours a day, five days a week, forty-one weeks a year, Jim found it easier to communicate with his boss through the language of jokes. He mostly found her a delight to work with professionally, but off-camera he didn't appreciate her biting wit that could sometimes insult guests or even regular crew members.

He related one story about one of their writers, Fat Phil, who once announced that he was on (another) diet, but this time he would see it through. To prove the fact, he offered a thousand-dollar bet that he would lose twenty pounds in two weeks. Joan took that bet and two weeks later collected. The poor man, three pounds heavier, claimed he was joking when, a fortnight later, Joan came to claim her winnings which were deducted from his paycheck that month.

The thing that most irked Backus was the billing, "the lifeblood of every actor," as he called it. As Joan owned the show and was its main powerhouse (star, unofficial gag writer, producer, unofficial director, etc.), the opening credit read "Starring Joan Davis with Jim Backus." That "with" made all the difference, placing Backus in second banana status. It was also an odd position for a straight man, who would essentially have a career as a featured comic actor later.

Like *I Love Lucy*, Joan's series was prop comedy that was difficult to do in a single take, and sometimes dangerous. A registered nurse was on the set at all times, and she didn't just sit around. Neither star used a double, even with some of the more complex stunts, resulting in one of the highest insurance rates for all of television.

Of course, as Backus rightly wrote, "Lucille Ball was to Joan Davis what Moriarty was to Sherlock Holmes." After seeing Ball photographed in front of a large mobile home for her new film *The Long, Long Trailer*, Joan requested a mammoth "portable" dressing room be constructed at the studio, which was so huge that part of a soundstage had to be knocked down to rebuild it around the massive ten-wheeled monster. Naturally, the wet bar and septic tank bidet made those thirteen-hour days pass quicker. The trailer still sat there long, long after *IMJ* left the air, finally demolished by the company that bought the studio, since they didn't have enough money to move it.

A rare radio photo of Lucille Ball and Joan together.

Among the props used were sometimes "guest stars," or the animals that were supposed to play a role, but sometimes they just didn't want to go by the script. One episode was supposed to have a lengthy chase of a turtle by the starving couple, only to end in their eating turtle soup from a hot water bottle. Perhaps the turtle didn't like the script. He just sat there.

Another time, even though Joan had once been bitten by a chimpanzee on a movie set, they were using one to play a medieval court jester in an *IMJ* dream sequence. But the bells on his hat and his rubber pants drove him crazy. He kept dropping his wand, too. Joan hated that chimp, becoming more heated as the animal wasted more and more film time. Finally, the director got the perfect take and yelled to print it. Joan may have been right about her constant, often abusive, talk on how much those little guys loved to bite: as she was saying her weary goodnights to Jim, the chimp came over and bit her on the naval. She was rushed to the hospital, screaming all the way, "What did I tell you? Those little ****s are poison! I'll die! I'll die! I just know it!" She was kept overnight after a tetanus shot, and slowly recovered, perhaps focusing all the poison out of her system by wishing that monster dead, because, three days later, the chimp died.

Never trust a monkey.

The stress of being the power behind a hit series was gigantic. Joan couldn't even get a different haircut if it didn't work into the plot of the next storyline: she wanted to get a new "Italian cut," so, it became the premise for one of the programs. But not before her blonde secretary, Jean Gordon, went for one first, to see how it would look.

She told *The New York Morning Telegraph*, "I've made a lot of movies under all sorts of conditions, but the work was never anything like this. For nine months a year you never stop. Every week they have me doing all sorts of things that call for using a tremendous amount of physical energy. But maybe this is good. I don't get all pent up inside, so I avoid the occupational disease of ulcers. If things do go wrong occasionally, I just explode for a few minutes and that keeps me in shape."

Would you marry this woman?

When doing some of those zany stunts, Joan would have a few of the wildest tried out by "some proxy character" because, as she honestly admitted, "if I get hurt, I've got to close up the store. We're never more than eight or ten films ahead, you see." In one episode that required a shelf full of dishes to bounce accidentally off her head, Joan was hesitant. "When I fingered the dishes, they were like a hunk of lead. I told the director we'd better try it on somebody else. With that, the assistant director, Joe DePew, scoffed that there was nothing to it. He stepped in to show me how harmless it was, and he almost knocked his brains out. He wasn't well for three weeks."

Knowing how to make the most of live-broadcast mistakes was the mark of a true professional, however, and one which Joan knew well from years of radio and stage work. "Comics rely a great deal on accidents. It was because of an accident that I became known as a pratfall comedienne, not by choice. I used to do slides on my heels, but one time I fell, and I got a much bigger laugh. From then on, I wrote it into the act."

Joan the housewife.

Those write-ins helped *I Married Joan* score some of its biggest yucks as well. On one show, Joan was supposed to be acting out the quotation "Ice cream has no bones" in a game of charades. To simulate bones, she kept feigning the rolling of dice so much that her waist slip vibrated off and fell to the floor. Instead of cutting the sequence, they worked the running gag into the story of her slip falling all through the show.

As production supervisor also, Joan admitted, "I'd rather shoot a complete episode in one day and get it over with. But it's worth it. You don't get returns from anything else like you do from TV. I was in Honolulu last year and a native woman put a lei around my neck when I landed; told me she sees me on TV in her grass hut. It's the fastest way of becoming a star, and the hardest. Now they're making the actor really work for the money. In the movies, if you film three minutes a day, it's considered good. I do 30 minutes a day."

Soon, to spend more time with her daughter, and to give Beverly an added boost to her career in front of millions of people, Beverly joined the cast of *IMJ* as Joan's little sister, a move that worked quite well, considering how much the

Barely even time to eat these days.

two looked and sounded alike. It also helped the demographics for more young viewers. Beverly added insight that just wasn't there before.

"The kids didn't like your show very much last night, Mother," Beverly explained after an episode involving a hot rod. "That joke was square. A hot rod has to be able to do fifty in low gear or it isn't any good. I know you're a little old-fashioned about these things, but if you're going to be solid with the kids, you've got to get hep." The following week, Joan hepped up by having Beverly sit in on a script meeting, incorporating a change. She continued to be sensitive to the reactions of her daughter and her crowd from then on.

Beverly said at the time, "When I was signed up to be my own mother's sister on the *I Married Joan* show, it didn't surprise me a bit. That sort of thing has been happening to me ever since I became Joan Davis's offspring.

"My biggest disappointment in life was when I was too young to play my mother's daughter in *If You Knew Susie.* The producer decided that the part needed a girl older than I was at that time. I wasn't too old to play my mother, though—as a child, of course—in *George White's Scandals.* Now I'm too old to play her daughter, so I'm playing her sister.

"I've seen my performances in Joan's new series for this season and from the way she looks and the way I look, I'll soon be able to play *her* mother."

Joan said at the time, "She's awfully good, but I can't get used to her calling me Joan. I flinch every time she does it. She has always called me Mother or Mommy.

"She sounds exactly like me. Same voice, same inflection. She can mimic anything I do, the takes, the falls, everything. On the first show they put too much makeup on her and she came out looking more like my mother than my daughter. She won't let them do that again."

Like mother, like daughter.

Joan wanted to keep looking young enough after 40 to keep up with the physical rigors of live slapstick comedy. She told the *Los Angeles Times*, "I like good food, but watch my weight. If I gain two or three pounds I go on a diet until I am back to normal. Staying young means concentrated effort. Wishing doesn't get you anywhere. I have no patience with people who keep talking about how much they want something but never do anything about getting it.

"'I wish I had your figure,' they say to me. And I always tell them, 'You could if you really wanted to.' Your figure can be corrected in so many ways. My problem was to have a more slender waist. I went about getting this the wrong way. I dieted strenuously and lost where I didn't want to: in my face. But I visited a famous health farm run by a beauty expert and they gave me a series of exercises. I did these at home for 10 minutes every night and morning and I went down two sizes in my waist measurements.

"Every woman, even if she is not in show business, has an obligation to her family and friends to keep in good shape. But look out for the excuses laziness will make you think up. Lots of people feel comfortable repeating the saying 'The only way to beat old age is to die young,' but I don't agree. You can stay young if you have a strong enough desire.

"You have to think young and you have to take care of your body. Keep it agile. It's lack of exercise, not age, that makes people stiff. And two days every month I go on a health kick. I give my body nothing but liquids. An M.D. who had studied yoga told me this. There is nothing like it for cleaning out your system—giving your digestive tract a rest. It's not easy, but I would not miss it—I feel rejuvenated.

"I've been using make-up since I was 3 so I have to be very careful that my complexion is really clean. First I use a cream and then I scrub with lots of soap and hot water."

"I wasn't so lucky," Beverly told the same paper. "I had what the doctor called adolescent skin. I tried X-rays and shots, but the thing that really helped me the most was to keep oily foods out of my diet because I had too much oil in my skin."

Beverly also felt the stress radiating from being cast in the public eye, but being able to work with her mother made up for the sacrifices. "I always promised Beverly a sister," Joan said at the time, "but neither of us ever imagined it would turn out to be me! Beverly's taller than I am—five feet six to my five, five-and-a-half. She has to wear low heels and crouch a bit, so she'll look shorter."

Beverly and her grandmother helped Joan with her weekly fan mail, sometimes sitting by the pool as poodles Piccolo (or Pierre) and Spanky madly barked at the reporters coming for another interview. Joan told one newsman, "It's a whole new phase of show business. I receive more than 500 letters a day. No movie star gets that. And even the most popular film there is, in its entire run, doesn't play to the same number of people that one top TV show can reach."

Chapter 13
Bev & The Dean

Bev had a much more active social life than her mother—she certainly had more time for it. One one-date beau was entertainer Sandy Singer. "My folks and I were at the Chez Paree, Chicago's answer to New York's Copa. Joan was dating a fellow my father knew. We all sat together, and Joan introduced me to Beverly, and set up our date for the next day. Sam Cowling of the *Breakfast Club* radio series lived across the street from us. I knocked on his door and asked if Don would be interested in interviewing Beverly. Sam said, 'Heck, yes.' So, our day started very early—we had to be at NBC, Studio A by 7:30 a.m. Bev and I went to breakfast after the show, because McNeal was too cheap to serve breakfast on the *Breakfast Club*! (They used to hold up signs as the opening theme played—'we don't serve breakfast'—'McNeal is too cheap,' etc.) We then headed for Wrigley Field, to watch a Cubs game. Afterwards, Beverly and I caught a cab to the Ambassador East Hotel, home of the Pump Room. It was Joan, her Chicago boyfriend, Beverly and me. Who do we run into—Victor Borge, a good friend of Joan's. Well, we all ended up having dinner together—Borge was an absolute riot! That's pretty much my day with Beverly Wills."

On January 10, 1952, Louella Parsons announced Beverly's engagement to CBS TV director William Bast; Beverly told the columnist after telling her sorority sisters at the Gamma Phi Beta house in Los Angeles' University of California. "I want you to know right away too," she told Parsons. "Of course, I'm going to finish school—I'm just a freshman. I've known Bill for a year and have been in love with him for *months*. Mother, who is in New York, telephoned and asked me not to marry until I had completed my education."

William Bast, later a writer for television, went out with Beverly for a few months, and gave a completely contrary account of his time with Joan than what the usual complimentary magazine stories ran. They were often exactly the same negative thoughts that ex-husband Lee Bamber would have: Joan was mean—both in temperament and financially, treated her mother shabbily, snapped at Bev constantly, and was petty and competitive. It was *not* the glowing family picture the studios wanted to paint. Bast and Bev went out for about six months, at which point James Dean, his roommate at the time, stole her away. This was even worse for Joan. She did not like the Dean kid. And her opinion could hardly improve when Dean, who, according to Bast, never picked up a golf club in his life, beat Joan at her favorite game their first time out.

Beverly's highest-profile relationship had come in 1951. The following is her detailed confession, as told to Helen Weller, in the magazine article, "I Almost Married Jimmy Dean," written just before his untimely death.

I was Jimmy Dean's girlfriend. We went steady for seven months, and at one time we talked about getting married. I loved Jimmy at that time and I understood him as few people did.

We met on a blind date about five years ago. He was a bashful boy behind big horn-rimmed glasses and his hair looked as though it hadn't been combed in weeks. When we were introduced, he merely said, "Hi," and stared at the floor. Finally we got into his car and drove to a shore picnic—and he hardly said a word. He was a little self-conscious about his car, not because it was beat-up looking, but because he couldn't whip any speed out of it. "Good old Elsie," he said with a wry kind of smile, stroking the wheel. "I call her Elsie because she's slow as a cow. I hate anything slow. I wish I could trade this in for a fast job." After that little speech, he clammed up and didn't say another word.

I thought he was pretty much of a creep until we got to the picnic, and then all of a sudden he came to life. We began to talk about acting and Jimmy lit up. He told me how interested he was in the Stanislavsky method, where you not only act out people, but things too.

"Look," said Jimmy, "I'm a palm tree in a storm." He held his arms out and waved wildly. To feel more free, he impatiently tossed off his cheap, tight blue jacket. He looked better as soon as he did, because you could see his broad shoulders and powerful build. Then he got wilder and pretended he was a monkey. He climbed a big tree and swung from a high branch. Dropping from the branch, he landed on his hands like a little kid who was suddenly turned loose. He even laughed like a little boy, chuckling uproariously at every little thing. Once in the spotlight, he ate it up and had us all in stitches all afternoon. The 'creep' turned into the hit of the picnic.

I learned that it was nothing for Jimmy to run through a whole alphabet of emotions in one evening, alternating sharply from low to high and back again, and no one could ever tell what mood would hit him. A couple of nights later, we went to a movie and during the picture Jimmy sat hunched forward, his chin cupped in his hands, looking something like that statue of the thinker. When I tried to whisper something to him, he shushed me up. He was so completely absorbed in the performance on the screen! Jimmy was still in this somber mood when we left, and when we got into his car he didn't say a word. Suddenly he said, "I feel like some music." He started to sing "Roll, Roll, Roll Your Boat."

I was beginning to see Jimmy every day now and I noticed that he always wore the same clothes, a blue jacket and gray slacks. Either that or a pair of jeans. That was all he owned.

Once he spilled coffee on himself and it left a stain on the slacks. He jumped up and was so mad at himself. I couldn't understand it, because Jimmy didn't seem to give a hoot about clothes.

"It's only a pair of pants," I said, "send it to the cleaners."

"That's just it," he said. "I can't even pay the cleaners, and I wanted to go to the studio tomorrow and see about a job."

Jimmy wanted more than anything else in the world to become an actor. But he couldn't get a job. It would almost kill him when he'd go out to see the casting directors and return with nothing. He never lost confidence in himself, but he was angry because no one else shared that confidence. He would come by and see me after a fruitless interview, and he'd be in a black mood. "The director said I was too short," he once mumbled savagely. "How can you measure acting in inches? They're crazy!"

They also told him he wasn't good-looking enough, and always that he wasn't the type. Usually, when the casting heads told him this, Jimmy would get so mad he'd insult the men right back!

I was doing a part in the radio version of *Junior Miss*, and Jimmy would sit in on the rehearsals and watch. One day, they needed a young man for one of the roles and Hank Garson, the director, asked me if my boyfriend could handle it. "Of course," I said happily.

I introduced Jimmy to Mr. Garson. "Have you ever done anything in radio?" asked the director. Any other actor, faced with such an opportunity, would have said yes, but not Jimmy. I think he was a little angry at the director for having let him sit around for so many weeks before offering him a job, and he wanted to show off. Anyway, Jimmy looked defiantly at Mr. Garson and said, "No." "Sorry," said the director, and walked away.

I ran after Jimmy. "Why did you say that?" I asked. "Why didn't you tell him you could do it? If you'd only been nice, he'd have given you a chance."

Jimmy was still stubborn. "I don't have to lie to get a job in radio. Either he can give me a chance because he thinks I can act, or he can take his old job."

But although he used to rub many people—unfortunately, important people—the wrong way because of his hurts and resentment, he could charm the birds off the trees when he wanted to.

My mother didn't share my enthusiasm for Jimmy, nor was my mother to blame. Jimmy had the knack of putting his worst foot forward when he was in the mood. I think it was the rebel in him. My mother—she's Joan Davis— was a success; he wasn't. Inside, Jimmy felt a little antagonistic toward many of the people who had achieved success in a profession where he couldn't stick his foot in the door.

He'd walk into our living room and promptly slump down in my mother's favorite armchair, his foot dangling over the side, and sat like that for hours without saying a word. The only action we'd see out of him was when he'd reach out for the fruit bowl and eat one piece of fruit after another until the bowl was empty. When my mother would walk in, Jimmy never stood up, never said *hello*. He just remained slouched in the chair, munching on the fruit and staring moodily into space.

At the dinner table, his behavior was usually the same. Jimmy was always hungry. He loved pot roast, so I tried to have it for him whenever he was over. He'd would down two helpings of the meat with that same morose expression on his face, and mother would squirm.

It was more than his manners that disturbed my mother. She was afraid we were becoming serious. By this time I was wearing Jimmy's gold football on a chain around my neck. We were going steady and my mother couldn't think of any boy who had a more uncertain future than Jimmy! She thought he was too wild and would never settle down.

My high school senior prom was coming up and, of course, I was going to take Jimmy. He was working as an usher at the time, and although he was in debt, he managed to put aside a few dollars every week so that he could rent a tuxedo. He asked me to go with him to the place where you rent these things, and when he saw all the dinner suits on racks he acted like a little boy in a candy store. He tried on one after another, and finally settled on a white jacket, black pants, dress shirt and bow tie. The rental on the whole works amounted to five dollars, and I don't think I ever saw Jimmy look happier.

"Imagine me in one of these things," he crowed, posing in front of a long mirror.

Although we sat out most of the dances—Jimmy didn't rhumba or jitterbug— he was in wonderful spirits the night of the prom. Some of the kids at school joined us and he laughed a lot and told funny stories. My mother stopped by with some friends for a few minutes, and even she was fascinated by Jimmy's personality that night. He jumped out of his chair when she came to our table and even helped her off with her stole. "Good heavens, I've never seen him like this before," said mother, flabbergasted but charmed.

The only other times I saw Jimmy that happy was when he was racing his motorcycle furiously. No matter how depressed he was, if Jimmy had a chance to get behind something that had terrific speed, he would laugh and come alive again.

When Jimmy learned that I had a little boat with an outboard motor, he was eager to try it out. Jimmy drove it around the Cove, the salt spray making his face and his glasses glisten. I thought he enjoyed it, but he was disappointed because he couldn't get my little boat with its ten horsepower motor to whip up any great amount of speed. After that little ride, which I thought would turn out to be such fun, Jimmy was in the dumps again.

I soon discovered that his moods of happiness were now far outweighed by his moods of deep despair. He was almost constantly in a blue funk. He still couldn't get an acting job and he was growing increasingly bitter. I hated to see Jimmy become so blue. When he was happy, there was no one more lovable. When he was depressed, he wanted to die.

These low moods became so violent that he began to tell me that he was having strange nightmares in which he dreamed he was dying. The nightmares began to give him a certain phobia about death. "If only I could accomplish something before I die," he once said despairingly.

Like a lot of kids who go steady, we began to talk about getting married. I was not yet eighteen and we both knew my parents would never give their consent, so we planned to wait until my eighteenth birthday, which was a couple of months off, and elope. I had saved some money from my radio work, and we thought we would go to New York where we hoped Jimmy could get a break in the theatre.

But the dream didn't last long. A couple of months later, I had moved to Paradise Cove, a beautiful spot way out at the beach, where I was to spend six months with my father—my parents are divorced. The first week Jimmy drove out the long distance he began to gripe. "It's such a long drive, I'm running out of gasoline. Why can't you meet me in Hollywood?"

But I felt at home at the beach. I was with a lot of happy kids whom I'd grown up with every summer, and we were having lots of fun. Somehow, in this happy-go-lucky atmosphere, surrounded by boys and girls who didn't seem to have a care in the world, Jimmy stuck out like a sore thumb. He wore the same blue jacket and gray pants, only they seemed even shabbier next to the tailored slacks and sports shirts the other fellows wore. The whole crowd was very cliquey, and when Jimmy came by they looked at him as though he didn't belong.

Jimmy was very sensitive and it hurt him very much to be looked down on. He sensed their patronizing attitude and withdrew deeper and deeper into a shell. I think he wanted to hurt them back, too. I've often wondered if he recalled this period in his life when he portrayed the sensitive feelings of the rejected youth in *Rebel Without a Cause*.

One afternoon, the fellows were playing football on the beach. Jimmy joined them. He used to be very intense about everything he did, particularly if he wanted to show off. The other fellows were playing casually, since they weren't wearing protective football gear, but Jimmy plunged into the game like a tiger. He was out for blood. He was very strong, anyway, and he tackled one of the fellows in pain and the rest of the fellows ran over to pull Jimmy off him. After that, the fellows labeled Jimmy a bum sport and wouldn't talk to him.

Jimmy was miserable. He felt like an outsider in his work; he felt like an outsider with this crowd. The resentment made him sink all the more into rebellious moods that even I couldn't understand.

At a dance at the Cove one night, Jimmy remained in this strange mood. When one of the boys cut in and tried to dance off with me, Jimmy saw red. He grabbed the fellow by the collar and threatened to blacken both his eyes. I should have realized that this was his way of paying back a member of the crowd who had hurt him. But I was embarrassed. I ran out to the beach, and Jimmy walked after me, scuffing angrily at the sand, complete misery on his face. We had an argument and I pulled his gold football off the chain.

A few days later, Jimmy called and told me that a friend was driving to New York and would give him a free ride. I was glad he called. I had been thinking of Jimmy ever since we broke off, and I realized more and more that this was a hurt and misunderstood boy. I wanted to remain his friend. I wished him luck.

A few months later my mother took me on a trip to New York. I had Jimmy's address. He was staying at the Y and I called him up. We met in Central Park and my heart went out when I saw Jimmy walk up in the same blue jacket and gray slacks. That meant that he still hadn't gotten a job. There was an air of bravado about Jimmy which soon crumpled when he told me that he hadn't been able to land a part in a show. He was depressed, and he was hungry, too. I insisted that I buy us both a spaghetti dinner and he took me up on it. I think it was the first square meal he had had since he left Hollywood to come to New York.

I told him I was engaged to be married, and he told me about a girl he had met in New York who was a lady bullfighter. I could see that he was fascinated by this colorful girl. He showed me a tiny matador sword which he wore in his lapel, and he had gone overboard on the subject of bullfighting.

Later, he walked me back to my hotel. Just before he left, he said, "I'm trying out for a part in a play tomorrow. It's a good, gutsy part. If I get it, I think this will be the break I've been waiting for. Maybe even Hollywood will sit up and take notice. I'll show them. If I don't get it," he paused, fingered the little sword in his lapel, and the familiar little smile played over his lips, "well, then I'll go to Mexico and become a bullfighter."

I kissed him on the cheek and wished him well, and then watched him walk down the street. He kicked at some stones like a little boy scuffing down the street, and he stopped under a lamppost to light a cigarette. Then he squared his shoulders, turned the corner and was gone.

He never did go to Mexico.

In 1952, at age 18, Bev eloped to Carson City, Nevada with Lee Bamber, a 25-year-old firefighter from Pasadena, California. Joan wasn't happy, cautiously commenting, "At 18, kids sure do think they know everything."

Bamber admitted to this author, "I was attracted to Bev because I was a poor nerd from the sticks, attracted by the glamor and glitter, certainly not by her looks. Pretty she was not, neither was her mother; they were about on par. When I moved to Los Angeles, I became a Pasadena fireman and I looked up a fraternity brother who was an archery fiend. He would go to an archery range, a miniature golf course on Hollywood Blvd. and practice, and I would tag along and play ping-pong since archery didn't appeal to me.

"There was a girl playing there that was quite good, so I challenged her and that led into a nightly meeting to play ping-pong. After about a week, after everything was shut down, my friend, the owners and I were sitting around B.S.ing, having a beer, and the owners were talking about their struggle to get enough business to make some money. One of them said it's too bad they couldn't get Joan Davis' daughter interested in investing in the place because that could lead to some more names for publicity. With that I asked, 'Does Joan's daughter come here?' They said, 'You dummy, you've been playing ping-pong with her for a week!' That led into a birthday interlude at her apartment that ended up in our eloping to Carson City. Joan learned of the marriage from an article written by Harrison Carroll in *The Hollywood Reporter*—a friend of Bev's had sold her secret for a $25 bird dog fee. Joan was *not* pleased.

"I believe the last time I saw Joan was when she and Danny Elman came to our duplex. Bev cooked the first meal of her life; Lamb Chops per Nina. Bev and I got in a fight over me drinking some booze that was supposed to be just for her mother. I handed her my wallet and told her go buy a replacement. She took the

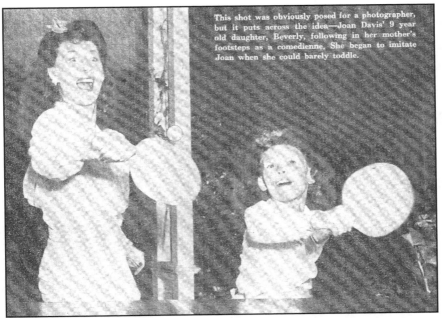

This shot was obviously posed for a photographer, but it puts across the idea—Joan Davis' 9 year old daughter, Beverly, following in her mother's footsteps as a comedienne. She began to imitate Joan when she could barely toddle.

Joan teaches Bev table tennis.

wallet and slapped me across the face with it. I just saw red. I guess she could see it in my eyes because she turned to get away from me and all I saw was her retreating ass, so I kicked it as hard as I could. She had a bruise on her butt for weeks. Needless to say, the dinner was a flop."

The marriage didn't last anyway. At age 20, she divorced Lee Bamber. Lee states, "I know this is fact because my brother and sister-in-law were there: Joan threw a birthday party for Bev for leaving me. Before that, Joan had insisted that she have our Pomeranian spaded since Joan's poodle got so horny while she was in heat. It killed the little Pom, which Bev just loved to death. They were notified the day of the birthday party and Joan immediately hit the booze. At the cutting of the cake, Joan took the whole cake and ground it into Bev's face, saying, 'This is for the years of misery you've caused me.' She stormed out of the room and went upstairs to her bedroom with Bev following. There was yelling and screaming and lots of insulting before they both came flying out the door, tumbling down the stairs with all the guests standing there in amazement. Several of the guests were important show people and reporters from the trade mags and newspapers. Joan was completely bombed and had nothing but insults for most of the people there.

"Divorce was very easy. I kept the bar [in Hollywood, which Bev had bought for Lee] and she got everything else, which was zilch. The car was the only thing of any value. I last saw Bev when she was in Salem, Oregon doing a state fair expo selling something with the husband she had at death. They got in a fight and she took a cab from Salem to Oregon City, where my mother lived. She arrived in the early morning so she spent the night there and got a hold of me later. We spent that day together, and the night, and I felt that with a little persuasion I could get her to stay. She had just inherited over a million bucks, so naturally I had to be interested, but after spending 24 hours with her, I couldn't wait to get her on a plane to L.A. You can't imagine how miserable a human being she was, particularly now that she was a millionaire."

Joan was happy for the separation from Bamber, but admitted to a magazine, "I'm a wonderful, wonderful mother, and an awful, rotten in-law. Not that I was bad. I didn't interfere. I was quite concerned, though. I wanted Beverly to finish school first. She graduated valedictorian from high school. I wanted her to go on those extra four years."

In July of 1954 Beverly married Army Lt. Alan Norton Grossman; she, 20, he, 22. They met several years previously on a blind date arranged by friends. The wedding took place in the Crystal Room of the swanky Beverly Hills Hotel at noon with Rabbi Edgar F. Magnin officiating. Si gave the bride away. The couple

Bev and Alan Grossman.

took off on an extended (probably 10-day) honeymoon in the Hawaiian Islands. It was reported that the couple would then reside in Fort Lewis, Washington, where Grossman was stationed with a field artillery battalion, and that Bev would give up her career. They wanted to make plans for a home after he completed his 15 months of Army service. But when the couple returned from the islands, those plans were never mentioned again and Mr. Beverly Wills appeared on an episode of *I Married Joan*.

In an article/interview given to *Pictorial Review*'s John Maynard, Grossman stated (in typical press release fashion): "It was not very long ago that Beverly Wills consented to be Mrs. Grossman, thus entitling me to my present status. Now it's fascinating in a way to contemplate that Joan Davis is my mother-in-law, and no other man can make that statement.

"I don't know how you think of mothers-in-law, what image the phrase connotes in your mind. Comic strips and nightclub emcees have done a lot to condition the public mind in this matter, and the consequences haven't given mother-in-law much of a break. As I always got it, she's an old battle-axe with a dim view of her daughter's taste in husbands, a mind like a steel trap and a mouth to match.

"That doesn't suit my mother-in-law at all. Mine does deep knee-bends and push-ups, and can vault a six-foot fence if she has to. She can peg a rock at a sapling and nail it from 50 feet.

Bev, Alan and Joan.

"Then there's something else: she walks and talks like Beverly—or should that read the other way around? Anyway, it's a quality I'll always forgive her for.

"For instance, I phoned Beverly one night. There was nothing specially reserved about my end of the conversation. You might even say I was the last word in tenderness, overflowing with good will and, not to put too fine a point on it, love. I think I capped it with the information that I carried her beautiful face before me day and night.

"'Thank you,' she said. 'Not only is it sweet of you to say so, but that's quite a load you're toting around. Do you want to talk to Beverly now?'

"Did I say they talked alike? I now say it again.

"My mother-in-law is not the brittle type, either, which is funny in a way, because Beverly is. Beverly can break a bone just reaching for the sugar. You can't dent Joan with a crowbar, not that I had it in mind. You've seen the shellackings my wife's doddering parent takes on TV. I think she's constructed of rawhide.

"She's a better golfer than Beverly but Bev can take her at table tennis when she's hot. One night Bev and I were slated for a party somewhere. We were late. Joan had only worked 11 hours that day and felt like tapering off with a little mild exercise. Table tennis, for instance. Davis vs. Wills for the championship of nothing.

"Be over in a minute, Alan boy. Sit down and imitate a referee.

"I can tell you the score today. It's not an easy one either: 21-19, 19-21, 29-27, 23-25, 43-all—and Davis the winner by default. Beverly couldn't lift the paddle anymore. Party? What party?

"Quite conceivably, Beverly and I will have progeny of our own one of these days. But just one factor makes it almost inconceivable. It would make Joan a grandmother.

"There is a real crazy bit of casting. How many grandmothers do you know who flip themselves behind the wheel of their car instead of bothering to open the door? How many stand on their head as a normal concomitant to keeping in shape? How many will you find who earn their living by such grand-matronly chores as diving off merry-go-rounds? Well, stick around. You may hear of one yet.

"Life with Joan as an in-law hasn't begun yet for me in earnest. That will have to wait until the Army discharges me. But what I have had of it makes me look forward to the rest. I don't anticipate many dull moments.

"And as for the mother-in-law jokes, they simply don't connect with Joan in the least. That's serious. She's not domineering or hostile or any of those things. In fact, she's a very good friend of ours—the very best we have.

"She dotes on Beverly, sure—why shouldn't she? You might even say, so do I. But she believes implicitly in letting us lead our own lives, stepping in to help only when she's asked. And the time may come soon when she will be.

"For example, say I get a leave and Beverly and I decide to spend it back home. And invite an officer as a houseguest. Whom do we get for him to make a forth? That's easy. Beverly says hold the fort, Ma. We'll be double-dating yet."

"I'm going to miss Bev this year," Joan told **Woman's Home Companion**, "now that she's married and with her husband, who is doing his service stint at Fort Lewis, Washington. Si and I were divorced 10 years ago so she and my parents are all the family I have. But you have to learn to be self-sufficient in this business. There isn't time even for the usual circle of friends. Bill Boyd used to be one of my closest friends. Along came his TV work and mine—we never see each other. That goes for so many old friends. And I don't make new friends easily. I'm shy offstage and people meeting me for the first time are disappointed. They expect me to be funny, and I am pretty funny, but who wants to work all the time?"

Alan Grossman appears on an *I Married Joan* episode.

Needless to say, Alan never wrote the article. Reality was quite different. He told this author that "we didn't see her that much. She paid for our honeymoon to Honolulu, but Joan never came over to see us. We went over to see her sometimes. She wasn't interested in being a grandmother at all. She was the most unhappy person I've ever seen in my life. She had a 2/3 acre on a golf course in Bel Air—paid. She had a paid-for house in Palm Springs, belonged to the Hillcrest Country Club. She had absolutely everything and she was so unhappy.

"Of course Beverly's father was even worse. Verbally abusive to Beverly, always tearing her down. I'm surprised Beverly grew up as well as she did with a pair like that raising her. We went to see Martha Raye once, because Beverly got us backstage to meet her, and she couldn't've been nicer. And I kept asking myself, 'Why couldn't Joan be like this?' She only used Bev in *I Married Joan* as publicity, unlike Lucille Ball who gave her kids a chance when they were in her show.

"During the last year of our marriage I taught elementary school, which I then did for 35 years. We had no big problems. Beverly liked to spend money if we had it. We went to Las Vegas once and she went through a couple hundred bucks in about an hour.

"Joan always dressed up in bright pastel colors—powder blues or pink—because she wanted to be the queen. I guess she wanted to be seen, that's what all actresses do. We went to a football game once and she was all powdered up. She was a nice looking woman in person, and didn't try to make herself pretty on screen.

"She had a little refrigerator in her bedroom with liquor in it. Joan liked to drink. She had a very large account at a local liquor store. She was a very unhappy person. Yet, in her house she must've had hundreds and hundreds of 78 rpm albums of all her old radio shows. Of course they all were destroyed in the fire.

"The last time I saw Joan, before my divorce from Bev, she was in a hotel someplace in Beverly Hills and she was sick. She called up and wanted Bev to come over, so I went over. She was in bed, in a nightgown and she was really drunk. I'll never forget this. She was so drunk she wanted me to put my two fingers down her throat to make her throw up. That just did it. I left. That was my last memory of Joan."

Chapter 14

I Never Married Joan

The New York Herald Tribune announced on February 3, 1955 that JOAN DAVIS TOO 'WORN OUT' TO DO TV SHOW NEXT SEASON. Her contract would expire on April 6 and she found it an ideal time to announce her retirement from television. After three years of tempest teapot spinning, the great squeaky voice asked to be released from her General Electric contract. With a Neilsen rating of 21.5 (Disneyland had 42.4 and Arthur Godfrey 32.2, so it wasn't bad), the electric company agreed.

More than one report states she was simply sunk by Disneyland, which *did* manage to sink anything that tried to race against it.

I Married Joan was canceled in 1955, and, according to Backus, Joan became a recluse from that moment on. At least, he and Henny never saw or heard from her again. But she did appear once at the Slate Brothers Theatre in Milwaukee, where Jim was performing. She was genuinely interested in his performance, laughing with sincerity, looking thinner, a little sadder. The last thing she said to Jim was, "Goodbye, Brad. Tell Henny I'm sorry."

During the *IMJ* run she had put her film career on hold, due to obvious time constraints. However, *Jungle Joan*, as *Variety* reported on August 5, 1953, was to have been her next picture for Columbia. The feature, as well as all films for that studio, was canceled by mutual consent. Perhaps she was again functioning as a producer on *Jungle Joan*, since she returned several thousand dollars to Columbia which had already been spent on work on the screenplay.

At least the TV reruns still brought in money, both for her and NBC and General Electric, to which she was still under contract. From May 1, 1956 to March 9, 1957 *IMJ* brightened up mornings—especially for Joan, who had leased syndication rights to NBC for $1.15 million. Yet the show failed to catch on in the same *big* way that *I Love Lucy* did. Joan was never happy with that.

With pictures and television both out of the way, and finally on the verge of retiring, Joan now had time to reinvent her social life, which had been practically on ice for years.

During the *IMJ* run, Joan had a six-year romance with Los Angeles steel executive Danny Elman (some reports claimed he was a Chicago business man),

On the town with Danny Elman, trying to catch popcorn

but even that fell through with her constant dedication to television. "In my eyes, Danny's tall, dark and handsome. But he's medium sized and bald." He was also a hobbyist painter, but with Joan gone much of the time, she half-jokingly remarked, "I've been replaced by still life." When he gave her an engagement ring, she told reporters, "It's so big I'll have to put my arm in a sling to wear it." After the sour dissipation of her first marriage and the constant public spectacle of having a private life, Joan wasn't eager for a sequel to her wedding picture. "Danny lives in the same apartment house as my secretary. This way I call her and find out where he is and when he's going. And as for my television show, he'd better watch it. I ask questions."

She told *Woman's Home Companion* that "being a comedienne doesn't hurt a gal with men. Men like wit; they aren't afraid of a funny gal. They relax; they don't think they're being pursued when they're pursued with jokes.

"It takes unselfish people to be involved with a woman who has as little free time as I have. The unselfish person in my life is Danny Elman. Danny's business is steel, but in addition, he's highly creative, a talented painter. He interested me in art, and now I'm taking an art-appreciation course by correspondence. Danny is painting a portrait of me. [Joan was supposedly also a talented painter.] I told him it was risky. I want it to look like me but if it looks too much like me, this can be the end of a beautiful friendship.

"It is Danny who gave me my white toy poodle, Pierre Prince of Pompey, and Pierre is about to take over the whole house. It's a lovely house in Bel-Air, a house you hanker for after years on the road. I'm always doing something over; I just finished having a big outside porch enclosed and fixed up like a Louisiana sidewalk café. For the price it cost, I call it my Louisiana Purchase. It may seem strange for me to have a large house and live in it alone, but after working in an ugly barn like our television stage all day, it's wonderful to go home to something beautiful. Imagine going home to a furnished room! Oh, the good old days when the towns were so small there was no hotel and you bunked in rooming houses. Good old days, pooh!"

Still on the town with Danny Elman in 1949.

In 1954, Beverly described the expensive Joan Davis estate to writer Cobina Wright: "That lawn is about as safe as a mine field. People keep tripping over the permanent croquet wickets that are cemented into the lawn, or they fall into the pitch-and-putt golf course laid out on the lawn." Cobina wrote, "Anywhere in the house a visitor is liable to stumble over fishing gear and the oak-panelled formal dining room could be described as 'gracious' if only it didn't have a billiard table set right smack in the middle of the floor, with a green-shaded light bulb swinging over it, and a business-like cue rack that stands against the wall, where any other woman would keep her sideboard full of precious china and silverware."

Joan had a lot of optimism when she signed up with ABC in 1956 for the pilot *Joan of Arkansas*, written and directed by Philip Rapp, who directed the first *I Married Joan* episode. (The entire pilot script is included in the book, *The Television Scripts of Philip Rapp*.) "This is it," she stated. "The first comedy-science-fiction show in TV. The humor is based on situations involving me with actual scientific experiments. It may get a little rough on me physically but I'm used to that from my slapstick experience in the past. Space travel and sputniks are in the news and our show should appeal to all groups and sexes. Throughout the series I'll be accompanied by psychologists, anthropologists and the like, who record my reactions to different and challenging situations."

The pilot failed to attract network interest.

After the death of *Joan of Arkansas*, Joan pretty much gave up the spotlight. "If show business has been good to me, it has also robbed me of many things. I'd have liked a college education, the chance to travel, and time for friends. Show business cost me my first beaux, and it eventually cost me my marriage.

"And I've been afraid all along that I just wouldn't be funny or pretty enough for the long-time bigtime. I've kept going on a mixture of gall, guts, and gumption. Faith, too—I've hung onto faith until now I realize every heartbreak has been a stepping stone.

"It's Father and I who do the talking about retiring. We're quite a pair, Dad and I. We're so alike, the same stance, the same sense of humor, same bronchitis, both smoke too much. And both of us keep saying we're going to quit working. About a year ago [1953] I gave him a real pitch. 'All right,' I said, 'retire. Sit around, make with the garden, relax, fish, do all the things you want to do.' I won. He retired—for two weeks."

TV and Danny Elman commitments out of the way, Joan started dating again. In 1956 she was keeping company with 33-year-old Harvey "Budd" Stock, Jr., a safety engineer (some reports named him as a publicist). "He's been proposing to me almost since the first day we met. I suppose we're going to be ribbed because of the differences in age, but I don't think that will make any real difference because we're in love." Joan was 49 at the time, and still an attractive woman, with her bleached blonde, shingle-styled hair, as shown in newspapers of the day.

Joan and Budd.

On April 7, 1957, the *Los Angeles Times* reported that Joan had that day become engaged to "29-year-old" Budd, and that the wedding would take place "in the very near future," Joan said. "I've known Budd for seven years, but have been going with him only since last Christmas. He's been proposing to me almost since the first day we met." The ceremony would have been earlier, she said, "but things kind of went wrong for us." First they went to Yuma, Arizona, but found that a new law required a three-day waiting period; then blood tests failed to arrive in the mail just the previous day.

They sounded like excuses. Especially since the engagement lasted two whole years. Until the incident.

On January 30, 1959, most newspapers (a greater number than had carried the engagement announcement, of course) reported that Joan had Budd (now listed as age 35 and a realtor) arrested for assault and battery the previous night. Apparently he gave her a slap that was much too hard to classify as a love tap, which resulted from an argument about her missing house keys (she didn't know if Budd had them or not). "We got into an argument," she told the press, "and he hit me in the face. He is very strong and when he slapped me it hurt my neck. I don't know whether he hit me with the side of his hand or his open palm, but it threw my neck out and it's very painful. My back's stiff, too. It's fortunate we were standing on the nice soft grass in the front yard, because that's where I landed. He just drove away. I got up off the lawn and went in to call the police."

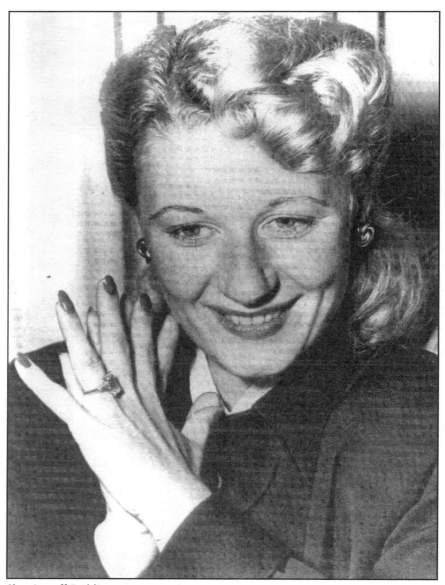

Showing off Budd's engagement ring.

After being taken in by the Palm Springs police and charged with assault and battery, Stock was released on $250 bail, making no comment to the press except when asked if this meant the engagement was off. "That's up to her," he said. Joan's melancholy replied was simply: "It looks that way, doesn't it?"

Joan dropped the charges on February 9, explaining, "I had everything to lose and nothing to gain" by prosecuting. "The engagement, however, definitely is off."

As usual, reports differed between newspapers. One claimed the argument began over a $25 loan Joan had made to Budd. Others listed the slap as a beating and that Stock knocked her down and kicked her, as well as using "either a rabbit punch or a judo blow [on the back of the neck]," as one police officer stated. Another version: the quarrel began during a drive back from her appearance on a Los Angeles television show. By the time they reached her house at two in the morning, a full-blown argument was well under way, at which point the actress was knocked sprawling into the front yard. Police later took photos of the indentations she made in falling and the strewn contents of her purse.

What really happened? We may never know for certain. Joan and Budd both had homes in the Palm Springs area and were to have been married in Riverside or Los Angeles, if all had gone well . . . It seemed that Joan was destined never to marry again.

It was a year of court dates. She also flew to Honolulu to testify in the $125,000 suit she filed against the Elizabeth Arden Sales Corporation, asserting that the company's beauty salon in the Royal Hawaiian Hotel had spilled bleach in her eyes three years previously, on May 18, 1954. The suit charged that Joan "suffered great shock and painful injury" when hairdresser John Gaul allowed bleach (touching up her blonde hair) to enter her eye. She claimed she was prevented from obtaining the needed rest and from completing sequences for *I Married Joan*. After winning $20,000 in damages, she was, of course, besieged by Hawaiian autograph seekers.

Nineteen Fifty-nine wasn't a good year. It was also the year her father, LeRoy Davis, died. She also suffered a possible nose fracture in mid-August, after a trip up the stairs in her home. Then Joan's home burned down.

Chapter 15
Quintuple Tragedy

On September 6, 1960, Joan was sitting in her living room, watching the Olympic Games on TV, completely unaware that the second story of her palatial, $135,000 Bel-Air home was in flames. Two unidentified "youths," whom Joan publicly thanked later, rushed up to her front door. They knocked heavily to inform her of the billowing smoke from her second-story that they had seen from across the street. Upon seeing the flames, Joan collapsed and had to be helped to a neighbor's home. After the fire department and a doctor were summoned, the rescuers left. Joan was put under sedation from the shock. Seven fire units from several different locations had to be called to battle the half-hour fight that finally extinguished the blaze, but not before three-fourths of her entire second floor (three bedrooms and a bathroom) was ruined, not counting significant damage to the first floor from heavy water and smoke damage. Firemen said the cause was possibly from a short circuit in electric wiring.

At home in Bel-Air.

Many of her possessions, including priceless family items, photos and scrapbooks, perished in the blaze. It left Joan in a weakened condition for months.

At eight o'clock on the night of March 22, 1961, Nina Davis called Dr. Max Levine to the Davis' Palm Springs home after Joan complained of back pains. He saw no indication of heart problems, but a half hour later Joan was rushed to a desert hospital by her mother. A spokesman told reporters the following morning, "She was conscious when she was admitted, and she seemed to be coming along fine. She was sleeping pretty well. And then at three this morning [March 23] she just went boom—just like that. She just stopped breathing." Nina remained at her beside at the time, along with a nurse and a Catholic priest. Joan Davis was 53 (some reports claiming 48).

Her body was transferred to a mortuary in Hollywood, where it lay in state for Thursday and Friday (May 25-26, 1961). The Rosary was recited on the 26th at the St. Paul the Apostle Church in West Los Angeles. Mass was held the next morning at 10:30, with Requiem Mass sung by Father Elwood Kaiser, who eulogized that Joan "was a woman who never wavered in her dedication to the highest goals in life." Several hundred people, including Hollywood celebrities, attended the service, while curious fans stood outside. Nina Davis was accompanied into the church by Si Wills. Her honorary pall bearers were attorney Paul Ziffren, theatrical agents Abe Lastfogel and George Gruskin, Richard Mack, accountant William Friedman and Bob Braun. Interment followed at the Holy Cross Cemetery in West Los Angeles. She was buried next to Mario Lanza and his wife, Betty, and perhaps fittingly, to the right of musical funnyman, Spike Jones.

Upon hearing of her death, Jim Backus stated that he was, "deeply, deeply shocked. She was the greatest female comedy talent we've ever had," which became a permanent part of her obituary as printed in nearly every newspaper. "She wasn't appreciated as much as she should have been. It will be extremely difficult for me to do my show tonight," he also stated. "I don't feel much in the mood."

The Davis family tragedy did not end with Joan's death.

Proceedings were begun by Beverly (Mrs. Beverly Colbert to the press, having just married Martin Colbert) and grandma Nina Davis contesting Joan's will, which left her $1 million estate to Si. Beverly's stance was that the divorced couple had reached a property/financial settlement in 1941, at which point a will had been made, which was nullified at the time of their 1947 divorce. Bev was told by her mother that when her divorce went through, Joan had destroyed the two wills (Joan's and Si's) in her possession. To further lay it on, Bev and Nina claimed that Joan had been unduly influenced into signing a later will, leaving Si the entire estate. They also stated that Si relinquished his right to share in his former wife's properties and that the will was fraudulently presented after Joan's death. Si claimed that he found the November 19, 1941-

document recently and petitioned the court on June 2, 1961 to admit it probate. Bev had a second, later will from 1956, written on the back of an envelope, leaving everything to her and her two sons.

Proceedings went to Superior Judge Clyde C. Triplett on June 26, 1961, with grandma Nina Davis accompanying Bev to court. Superior Court Judge Newcomb Condee actually presided, giving the unwelcome news that the will signed "Joan Davis" and dated "Friday, August 1956" did not appear to be witnessed and lacked the necessary elements—the full month, date and year.

The pencilled will read: "I Joan Davis leave to Lorena Watts [her maid] $10,000, $10,000 to my mother, $10,000 to my father and the rest to my grandson and daughter providing it does not go to my son-in-law, Alan Grossman."

Before the Judge made a final ruling, Si filed suit against Beverly to have the 27-year-old removed as special administratix of Joan's wealthy estate, citing that she did not have the business sense to oversee such holdings. Superior Judge Newcomb Condee denied the request, stating that the court should appoint the executor named in the will, attorney Warren Jefferson Davis, or a neutral party.

After more than three months, an out-of-court settlement was finally reached at the end of September 1961, at which point Bev told reporters, "I still love my father and I'm glad the matter is over." From the $1 million estate, Si was to receive the late star's Palm Springs home, "one of her business ventures" there, a car, and an "undisclosed" amount of cash (which some papers disclosed to be $52,000). Bev would retain the rest—the bulk of the estate.

Beverly continued her acting career, her most visible role being in 1959's classic *Some Like It Hot*. She had also been a regular on Barbara Whiting's radio show, *Junior Miss*, appeared in the television pilot *Shape Up Sergeant*, and took part in the stage revue *Chips Off the Old Block* at the Los Angeles Statler Hilton Hotel. But being a wealthy woman now gave her much less incentive to build up her career.

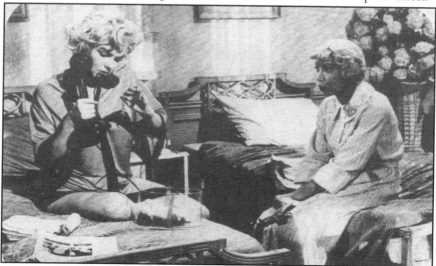

With Marilyn Monroe in *Some Like It Hot*, 1959.

Unfortunately, the Davis curse struck again. Beverly's smoking in bed seemingly caused a fire to break out in her Palm Springs home in the early hours of the morning of October 24, 1963. The blaze quickly moved from the master bedroom to the entire house, killing 70-year-old Nina Mae Davis, and Beverly's two young sons, Guy (age 7) and Larry (age 4). The coroner's office listed the official cause of death for Beverly as smoking in bed.

Larry (left) and Guy Grossman.

Early reports indicated that Nina and Guy were awakened by the fire in their adjacent bedroom and rushed into the master bedroom to help Bev and Larry escape. Firemen rushed to the scene while the house was still ablaze, quickly extinguishing flames that had leaped to the empty bedroom, though the rest of the house was not burned. Next-door neighbor Jack Schumer (who, as one news report stated, called the fire department at one in the morning) and firemen attempted to enter the master bedroom, but were unable to enter. Another neighbor, artist O.E.L. Davis heroically tried to make it to that bedroom also, looking through several rooms before being forced to retreat. Smoke or time kept him from finding the right door.

Firemen stated that even if the family had been found at 1:10 or 15 minutes before they had been called, they probably would have been found dead anyway, as there were indications that the fire had been smoldering for two hours before they arrived.

The charred bodies were found only after the firemen put out the blaze.

Nina was found on the floor at the end of the bed, her arms wrapped around her 7-year-old grandson. 4-year-old Larry was found laying across Bev's lap on the bed.

It was a Wednesday when the fire occurred. Husband Martin Colbert had left home at 7:00 that night to spend the night in Los Angeles on business. Before leaving, he dropped the family dog (a large French poodle) off at the vet's, and was going to pick it up the next day when he arrived home. One fireman commented after the fact, "The poodle is a great watchdog. She barks at the least thing. If the dog had been home, this wouldn't have happened, I'm sure."

Beverly.

The mass death began an interesting estate problem. In the event of Bev dying first, the estate would revert to her sons; if they died, it would all go to their father, Alan Grossman, now a Ventura County school teacher. If the sons died first, the estate would go to "motorcycle dealer" Martin Colbert. The Riverside County Coroner's office stated that they presumed all four deaths occurred within a matter of seconds of one another. Deputy coroner Don Mabbitt stated, "My office, of course, is not concerned with the order of death, but primarily the cause. It is my understanding that the physician conducting the autopsies has been requested to attempt to determine the order of deaths." Going back to try to establish the events of that terrible night, Assistant Fire Chief Warren Empy was questioned again. He stated that he believed that Nina and her oldest grandson, Guy, were both awakened by the smell of smoke, and that they made their way simultaneously to the master bedroom where Bev slept. Opening the door to this room may have caused a back-draught which then caused a minor explosion, blowing out the windows in the bedroom. The oxygen from the blown-out windows may have fanned the smoldering fire, trapping the four people in a hellish blaze.

Bev's holographic will left most of the estate to her two sons, grandmother and second husband Grossman. Martin Colbert was to receive $10,000 in cash and most of her personal belongings one year after her death. Nina was willed $25,000 in a trust fund. As everyone died at once, the will lost its meaning.

Even though newspapers reported that pathologist John Roos said it was probable that Nina Davis was the first to succumb to the fire, Superior Judge Merrill Brown later ruled that there was not sufficient evidence to prove anything but a simultaneous death. According to Roos, chemical and physical tests showed this sequence of death: Nina (heart attack), Larry (smoke inhalation), Beverly (smoke inhalation), and Guy (choked to death). Roos measured the amount of carbon monoxide in their blood, which gave him the order of death; there was more in Guy's blood than the others, indicating he lived long enough to breathe in more fumes.

Nina had moved in with the Colberts four months before the fire. She and Bev shared a service: the rosary was recited on Sunday, October 27, 1963 at the Palm Springs Mortuary chapel, followed by a requiem mass at 11:00 the following Monday morning at Our Lady of Solitude Catholic Church in Palm Springs. Arrangements for private grave-side services for Larry and Guy Grossman were made by their father, following a Jewish service at Hillside Memorial Park.

Credits

FILM

1935	WAY UP THAR (SHORT)(EDUCATIONAL)
1935	MILLIONS IN THE AIR (PARAMOUNT)
1937	THE HOLY TERROR (20TH CENTURY-FOX)
1937	TIME OUT FOR ROMANCE (20TH CENTURY-FOX)
1937	NANCY STEELE IS MISSING (20TH CENTURY-FOX)
1937	WAKE UP AND LIVE (20TH CENTURY-FOX)
1937	YOU CAN'T HAVE EVERYTHING (20TH CENTURY-FOX)
1937	SING AND BE HAPPY (20TH CENTURY-FOX)
1937	ANGEL'S HOLIDAY (20TH CENTURY-FOX)
1937	THE GREAT HOSPITAL MYSTERY (20TH CENTURY-FOX)
1937	THIN ICE (20TH CENTURY-FOX)
1937	ON THE AVENUE (20TH CENTURY-FOX)
1937	LIFE BEGINS IN COLLEGE (20TH CENTURY-FOX)
1937	LOVE & HISSES (20TH CENTURY-FOX)
1938	SALLY, IRENE & MARY (20TH CENTURY-FOX)
1938	JOSETTE (20TH CENTURY-FOX)
1938	MY LUCKY STAR (20TH CENTURY-FOX)
1938	HOLD THAT CO-ED (20TH CENTURY-FOX)
1938	JUST AROUND THE CORNER (20TH CENTURY-FOX)
1939	TAILSPIN (20TH CENTURY-FOX)

1939	DAY-TIME WIFE (20TH CENTURY-FOX)
1939	TOO BUSY FOR WORK (20TH CENTURY-FOX)
1940	FREE, BLONDE & 21 (20TH CENTURY-FOX)
1940	MANHATTAN HEARTBEAT
1940	SAILOR'S LADY (20TH CENTURY-FOX)
1940	FOR BEAUTY'S SAKE (20TH CENTURY-FOX)
1941	SUN VALLEY SERENADE (20TH CENTURY-FOX)
1941	HOLD THAT GHOST (UNIVERSAL)
1941	TWO LATINS FROM MANHATTAN (COLUMBIA)
1942	YOKEL BOY (REPUBLIC)
1942	SWEETHEART OF THE FLEET (COLUMBIA)
1943	HE'S MY GUY (UNIVERSAL)
1943	TWO SENORITAS FROM CHICAGO (COLUMBIA)
1943	AROUND THE WORLD (RKO)
1943	SHOW BUSINESS (RKO)
1944	BEAUTIFUL BUT BROKE (COLUMBIA)
1944	KANSAS CITY KITTY (COLUMBIA)
1945	SHE GETS HER MAN (UNIVERSAL)
1945	GEORGE WHITE'S SCANDALS (RKO)
1946	SHE WROTE THE BOOK (UNIVERSAL)
1948	IF YOU KNEW SUSIE (RKO)
1949	MAKE MINE LAUGHS (RKO)
1949	TRAVELING SALESWOMAN (COLUMBIA)
1950	LOVE THAT BRUTE (20TH CENTURY-FOX)
1951	THE GROOM WORE SPURS (UNIVERSAL)
1952	STRIP TEASE GIRL (MACK-SONNEY ENTERPRISES)
1952	HAREM GIRL (COLUMBIA)
1963	THE SOUND OF LAUGHTER (DOCUMENTARY)

Radio

1941–July 1, 1943	The Rudy Vallee Show
July 8, 1943–June 28, 1945	The Sealtest Village Store
September 18, 1943	Fall Parade of Stars
December 11, 1943	The National Barn Dance
April 18, 1944	Time to Smile (Eddie Cantor)
September 3, 1945–June 23, 1947	Joanie's Tea Room
September 22, 1945	Biggest Show in Town
October 11, 1947–July 3, 1948	Joan Davis Time
July 4, 1949–August 22, 1948	Leave It to Joan
September 9, 1949–March 3, 1950	Leave It to Joan
July 3, 1950–August 28, 1950	Leave It to Joan
December 3, 1950	The Big Show
February 11, 1951	The Big Show
April 1, 1951	The Big Show
April 22, 1951	The Big Show
November 4, 1951	The Big Show
December 30, 1951	The Big Show
January 6, 1952	The Big Show
February 10, 1952	The Big Show
February 17, 1952	The Big Show

TELEVISION

DECEMBER 4, 1951   LET'S JOIN JOANIE (PILOT) (CBS)

I MARRIED JOAN (NBC) (98 EPISODES)
OCTOBER 15, 1952–APRIL 6, 1955

SEASON 1:

OCTOBER 15, 1952	PILOT
OCTOBER 22, 1952	CAREER
OCTOBER 29, 1952	BALLET
NOVEMBER 5, 1952	JITTERBUG
NOVEMBER 12, 1952	CRIME PANEL
NOVEMBER 19, 1952	BRAD'S CLASS REUNION
NOVEMBER 26, 1052	HUNTING
DECEMBER 3, 1952	JOAN'S CURIOSITY
DECEMBER 10, 1952	BIRTHDAY
DECEMBER 17, 1952	BAZAAR PIE
DECEMBER 24, 1952	DREAMS
DECEMBER 31, 1952	ACROBATS
JANUARY 7, 1953	BAD BOY
JANUARY 14, 1953	CIRCUMSTANTIAL EVIDENCE
JANUARY 21, 1953	UNCLE EDGAR
JANUARY 28, 1953	MOOSEHEAD
FEBRUARY 4, 1953	FIREMAN
FEBRUARY 11, 1953	MEMORY
FEBRUARY 18, 1953	DRAFTBOARD
FEBRUARY 25, 1953	OPERA
MARCH 4, 1953	SHOPPING
MARCH 11, 1953	THE STAMP
MARCH 18, 1953	LITTLE GIRL
MARCH 25, 1953	DIET
APRIL 1, 1953	MODEL
APRIL 8, 1953	LATENESS
APRIL 15, 1953	THE EVICTION SHOW
APRIL 22, 1953	THE RECIPE
APRIL 29, 1953	REPAIRS
MAY 6, 1953	SECRETS
MAY 13, 1953	THE ARTIST SHOW
MAY 20, 1953	THE THREAT

SEASON 1 (CONTINUED):

MAY 27, 1953	COUNTRY CLUB
JUNE 3, 1953	THEATRICAL CAN-CAN
JUNE 10, 1953	NEIGHBORS
JUNE 17, 1953	TALENT SCOUT
JUNE 24, 1953	HONEYMOON
JULY 1, 1953	BUSINESS EXECUTIVE
JULY 8, 1953	BRAD'S BROKEN TOE

SEASON 2:

OCTOBER 14, 1953	BRAD'S MUSTACHE
OCTOBER 21, 1953	FIRST LIE
OCTOBER 28, 1953	FURNITURE QUICK CHANGES
NOVEMBER 4, 1953	SISTER PAT
NOVEMBER 11, 1953	TROPICAL FISH
NOVEMBER 18, 1953	MISSING FOOD
NOVEMBER 25, 1953	INITIATION
DECEMBER 2, 1953	BEV'S BOYFRIEND
DECEMBER 9, 1953	LOST CHECK
DECEMBER 16, 1953	THE SHOTGUN
DECEMBER 23, 1953	MUSICAL
DECEMBER 30, 1953	DOUBLE WEDDING
JANUARY 6, 1954	SUPERSTITION
JANUARY 13, 1954	BARBECUE
JANUARY 20, 1954	MOTHERS-IN-LAW
JANUARY 27, 1954	MABEL'S DRESS
FEBRUARY 3, 1954	MONKEYSHINES
FEBRUARY 10, 1954	BEV'S MISTAKEN MARRIAGE
FEBRUARY 17, 1954	MISSING WITNESS
FEBRUARY 24, 1954	ANNIVERSARY MEMO
MARCH 3, 1954	DENTED FENDER
MARCH 10, 1954	MOUNTAIN LODGE
MARCH 17, 1954	HOME OF THE WEEK
MARCH 24, 1954	POP RETIRES
MARCH 31, 1954	CHANGING HOUSES
APRIL 7, 1954	JEALOUSY
APRIL 14, 1954	GET RICH QUICK
APRIL 21, 1954	MASQUERADE
APRIL 28, 1954	THE MILKMAN COMETH
MAY 5, 1954	JOAN'S CURIOSITY (RERUN)

MAY 12, 1954	TALENT SCOUT (RERUN)
MAY 19, 1954	PREDICTIONS
MAY 26, 1954	BRAD'S BROKEN TOE (RERUN)
JUNE 2, 1954	BEV'S BOYFRIEND (RERUN)
JUNE 9, 1954	BRAD'S INITIATION
JUNE 16, 1954	CIRCUMSTANTIAL EVIDENCE (RERUN)
JUNE 23, 1954	CONFIDENCE
JUNE 30, 1954	DOUBLE WEDDING (RERUN)
JULY 7, 1954	JOAN'S HAIRCUT

SEASON 3:

SEPTEMBER 29, 1954	NEW HOUSE
OCTOBER 6, 1954	PARTY LINE
OCTOBER 13, 1954	WALL SAFE
OCTOBER 20, 1954	ALIENATION OF AFFECTIONS
OCTOBER 27, 1954	BOMBAY DUCK
NOVEMBER 10, 1954	DANCING LESSONS
NOVEMBER 17, 1954	TWO ST. BERNARDS
NOVEMBER 24, 1954	MANHOLE COVER
DECEMBER 1, 1954	THE FARM
DECEMBER 8, 1954	HOME MOVIES
DECEMBER 15, 1954	GUN MOLL
DECEMBER 22, 1954	CRAZY TOES SMITH
DECEMBER 29, 1954	JOAN PLAYS CUPID
JANUARY 5, 1955	THE WEDDING
JANUARY 12, 1955	THE MAID
JANUARY 19, 1955	MONEY IN THE SHOTGUN
JANUARY 26, 1955	EYE GLASSES
FEBRUARY 2, 1955	THE ALLERGY
FEBRUARY 9, 1955	LIEUTENANT GENERAL
FEBRUARY 16, 1955	THE LETTER
FEBRUARY 23, 1955	LADIES PRISON
MARCH 2, 1955	THE LADY AND THE PRIZEFIGHTER
MARCH 9, 1955	HOW TO WIN FRIENDS
MARCH 16, 1955	THE COWBOY
MARCH 23, 1955	THE JAIL BIRD

June 25, 1954	Campbell Television Soundstage ("The Psychopathic Nurse") (NBC)
1958	Joan of Arkansas (pilot)
September 11, 1960	The Chevy Mystery Show ("Blind Man's Bluff") (NBC)

Beverly Wills Credits

Films

1938	Anesthesia (short)
1945	George White's Scandals
1948	Mickey
1948	Raw Deal
1952	Skirts Ahoy!
1953	Small Town Girl
1954	The Student Prince
1959	Some Like It Hot
1961	The Ladies Man
1963	Son of Flubber

Index